Praise for
In Search of a Prophet

"Paul-Gordon Chandler takes us on a profound spiritual journey into the life and work of one of the most famous and beloved poets, Kahlil Gibran, showing us how this timeless poet is a much-needed guide for our times. In his hands, Kahlil Gibran becomes an intimate friend."
—Reza Aslan, author of *An American Martyr in Persia:
***The Epic Life and Tragic Death of Howard Baskerville*, *No god**
but God* and *Zealot: The Life and Times of Jesus of Nazareth

"Paul-Gordon Chandler has done us a great service by writing this wonderful book. Part travelogue through the many places Kahlil Gibran lived, part journey through the artist's great works, it all comes together in a way that gives us powerful glimpses into the inner life of a spiritual giant."
—Eboo Patel, Founder and President of Interfaith America,
author of *We Need To Build: Field Notes for Diverse Democracy*

"There are certain places you should visit before you die, and to enjoy them best, you need a guide who knows them well. Similarly, there are certain writers you should read before you die, and you'll enjoy them even more with an experienced guide beside you. Kahlil Gibran is such a writer, and Paul-Gordon Chandler is such a guide. Gibran, assisted by Chandler, will introduce you to a great land that lies within you."
—Brian D. McLaren, author of *The Great Spiritual Migration*

"An inspiring and vivid exploration into the all-embracing spirituality of Kahlil Gibran. Chandler takes us on a journey into the inner and outer world of a man who defied religious and cultural boundaries to assert a vision of an underlying humanity and faith that all people share, free of dogma. This original and revealing account of Gibran's life and work is timeless, sharing with us profound wisdom that can guide us through the challenges of our world today. A modern classic of spirituality."
—The Rev. Dr. Serene Jones, President and Johnston
Family Professor for Religion and Democracy at
Union Theological Seminary in the City of New York

"Paul-Gordon Chandler is a curious wanderer, a man of spiritual depth and refreshing insight. His journey into Kahlil Gibran's life and timeless teachings offers solace and shelter in our divided and troubled times."
—Jeffrey Fleishman, foreign and national editor at the
Los Angeles Times, and author of *Shadow Man: A Novel*

"*In Search of a Prophet* is a profound look at Kahlil Gibran's prophetic voice for peace and reconciliation during his lifetime. Paul-Gordon Chandler movingly demonstrates how Gibran, through his life and writings, issued a timeless call to respect all peoples and their religious traditions equally, thereby serving as an indispensable guide for our times."

—Ambassador Rabbi David N. Saperstein, former US Ambassador-at-Large for International Religious Freedom

"Here Paul-Gordon Chandler artfully traces the contours of Khalil Gibran's life—a life which transcended so many of the divides we human beings erect among ourselves. In a world increasingly fraught with voices calling us toward power and away from each other, this book arrives as a balm and an incitement to continue the important work of healing the world."

—The Rev. Dr. Amy Butler, former Senior Minister, Riverside Church, New York

"Paul-Gordon Chandler brilliantly captures the universal spirituality of the beloved poet Kahlil Gibran as we journey with him to discover how the Levant, his birthplace—the land of Moses's Sacred Valley, Jesus's Mount of Olives, and Mohammad's mosque of Al Aqsa—and early disappointments influenced his art and poetry. *In Search of a Prophet* is revelatory and a true inspiration for those seeking to build bridges, not walls."

—Imam Mohamad Bashar Arafat, president, Islamic Affairs Council of Maryland and Civilizations Exchange and Cooperation Foundation

"In this deeply spiritual look at the life of Kahlil Gibran, Paul-Gordon Chandler opens us to a voice more relevant to our times than when his work appeared years ago. Chandler's biography rings with the same grandeur and deep insight present in Gibran's poetry, and it is pleasant to read and nourishing to digest. With our world so deeply suspicious and divided, Chandler's look at Gibran offers us a biography—and a spirituality—that displays a vision of our common humanity. It is a great inspiration during times like these."

—The Rev. James Winkler, former president and general secretary, National Council of Churches

IN SEARCH OF
A PROPHET

A Spiritual Journey with Kahlil Gibran

PAUL-GORDON CHANDLER

Foreword by Bishop Michael B. Curry

ROWMAN & LITTLEFIELD
Lanham • Boulder • New York • London

Published by Rowman & Littlefield
An imprint of The Rowman & Littlefield Publishing Group, Inc.
4501 Forbes Boulevard, Suite 200, Lanham, Maryland 20706
www.rowman.com

86-90 Paul Street, London EC2A 4NE

British Library Cataloguing in Publication Information Available

Library of Congress Cataloging-in-Publication Data Available
Names: Chandler, Paul Gordon, author.
Title: In search of a prophet : a spiritual journey with Kahlil Gibran / Paul-Gordon Chandler.
Description: Lanham : Rowman & Littlefield, 2017. | Includes bibliographical references and index.
Subjects: LCSH: Gibran, Kahlil, 1883-1931. | Authors, Arab—Lebanon—Biography. | Authors, Arab—United States—Biography.
Classification: LCC PJ7826.I2 (ebook) | LCC PJ7826.I2 Z587 2017 (print) | DDC 811/.52 [B]—dc23
LC record available at https://lccn.loc.gov/2017010944

ISBN: 978-1-5381-0427-9 (cloth : alk. paper)
ISBN: 978-1-5381-7542-2 (pbk. : alk. paper)
ISBN: 978-1-5381-0428-6 (ebook)

∞™ The paper used in this publication meets the minimum requirements of American National Standard for Information Sciences—Permanence of Paper for Printed Library Materials, ANSI/NISO Z39.48-1992.

To my daughter and son, Britelle and Treston,
who are truly *le choix du roi*,
whose presence in my world
brings sheer joy, beauty, and inspiration

For I know in my heart that the Supreme Poet wrote but one poem.

—KAHLIL GIBRAN, *SAND AND FOAM*

Kahlil Gibran, *Sand and Foam,* in *The Collected Works* (New York: Alfred A. Knopf, 2007), 218.

CONTENTS

Foreword

B EFORE READING THIS BOOK, my only real knowledge of Kahlil Gibran was the poem from his bestselling book *The Prophet,* often read at weddings in the 1970s and 1980s and frequently caricatured. What that limited knowledge didn't reveal was the fascinating story of Gibran's life, the depth of his convictions, the breadth of his spirituality, and the gift of his wisdom. This remarkable book by Paul-Gordon Chandler shares with us Gibran's spiritual journey, revealing the power of his wisdom and passing on to us a profound gift for our day.

In so many ways, Kahlil Gibran, one of the most profound figures to have existed in the last century, is increasingly relevant for our times. While he was a prophetic voice during his own lifetime, the message of his life and work is even timelier today. Certainly, heeding his wisdom would go a long way toward healing our world.

In Search of a Prophet is much more enriching than a traditional biography of Gibran's life. I was fascinated to learn of the scope of his spiritual influence worldwide, both in terms of his reach geographically and the diversity and breadth of groups that have been blessed by his writings. It is clear to me why his works continue to speak so powerfully a hundred years after his bestselling book *The Prophet* was first published, which brought him global renown.

First of all, people today are hungry for a connection with the Transcendent. There is a profound desire for a spirituality without dogmatism, that enables one to stay centered and whole, where the divine in us is fed. Finding a way to powerfully communicate a nonsectarian version of spirituality was something that weighed heavily on Gibran. Even though he grew up in a Maronite Catholic Christian family in Lebanon, he went beyond organized religion to the core of a spirituality that was inclusive and all-embracing.

This book looks deeply into Gibran's inner spiritual formation and immerses the reader in his writings and the environments that shaped him. Gibran was preoccupied during his entire life with the depths that he knew the spirit of humanity was able to plumb. And it seems the deeper he went, the wider his embrace became. The depth of Gibran's spiritual journey led to an extraordinary breadth of spirit in which he experienced the oneness of humanity. The reservoirs he had cultivated in "the deep" gave him the capacity to go "wide." Arising from his faith journey, a spirituality emerged over time that transcended all cultures and traditions.

Consequently, Gibran felt called to create work that echoed what he believed was the spirit of the great majority of people, and he wove this passionate intent into the core of his writing. As a result, his spiritual search and discovery, as expressed in his words, resonates with many in our world today. His voice is timeless—a guiding spirit at a time when people are much more interested in spirituality than institutional religion.

Secondly, Gibran found himself increasingly interested in Jesus. Recently, the church I am associated with decided to ask the wider culture, both religious and non-religious, what they think of Jesus. We contracted with a global marketing group that does this kind of research. They conducted a comprehensive poll that provided a snapshot into the American population across all races, ethnic groups, religious bodies, political parties, and geographical territories. And 84 percent of the population said that Jesus is an important spiritual figure worth listening to—across all groups: Democrats, Republicans, independents, liberals, conservatives, religious, non-religious, Christian, Jewish, Muslim, Sikh, Hindu, no religion. Everybody. Black, white, everybody. Eighty-four percent of the people surveyed across the board found Jesus attractive and that there was something compelling about him. However, when they were asked about Christianity or the Church, the responses were quite discouraging. So, while Jesus is in, it is clear there is a gap between Jesus and institutional Christianity.

Gibran helps us close that gap between Jesus and his way of love to a wider culture, to those who aren't interested for whatever reason in religion. As Gibran journeyed spiritually, he sought to sift through the religious trappings of his own faith tradition, and he found himself looking deeply for its core essence. In so doing, he discovered the figure of Jesus in a new way. He came to see the person of Jesus beyond the Christian religion as someone whose life and teachings were for all humanity. Gibran saw Jesus as an all-embracing figure and was enraptured by his character. He was able to separate the Jesus of history from the Jesus of religion (i.e., Christianity), in which he was raised.

Hence, the opportunity to write about Jesus's life became an aspiration for Gibran. I was amazed to learn that the longest and last book Gibran wrote before he died was about Jesus, titled *Jesus the Son of Man*. In it, he delivers an enthralling picture of the essence of Jesus through the eyes and voices of individuals during the time of Jesus, some historical and others fictional. Gibran presents Jesus through a fresh lens that allows us to see that Jesus was all about the way of love, compassion, tenderness, forgiveness, kindness, and mercy.

Lastly, Gibran teaches us throughout his writings about the "way of love." Certainly, the most profound truth I've learned in my own spiritual journey is that the way of love is needed more than anything else in our world. The way of love is powerful, transformative, free, and freeing to all. Love builds; the opposite destroys. And real love is not soft, sweet, and sentimental. Real love seeks what is truly good, just, kind, and compassionate. It can often seem that our world right now is built on selfishness, indifference, and even hatred. Very often, it doesn't look good.

Yet, we are all called to live the way of love. It is only love that can stop the madness. And real faith dares us to believe that, in the end, love wins. Love is the way. Yet, none of us has the capacity to walk the way of love alone. We need spiritual energy to be able to connect with the source of love that is bottomless and endless—which is God's love. As Gibran writes, "God has given to your spirits wings to soar aloft into the realms of love and freedom."

Gibran's spiritual journey saw him mature into someone with a graciousness toward all that reached across the divides of humanity, building bridges of love. Gibran wrote, "Kindness is the shadow of God in man." And as a result, he was determined to tear down walls of injustice, advocating for freedom within and without for all people.

This book opens to us Gibran's spiritual journey of depth and breadth, offering our day much-needed wisdom and guidance. And it can't help but challenge us all. Gibran's words continue to reverberate in hearts and souls, stirring the reader, whoever they may be, to live deeply, reaching across the divides that surround us in love. I encourage you to read this book with an open heart, allow room for transformation and embrace the way of love.

—Bishop Michael B. Curry

Preface

S INCE THIS BOOK WAS FIRST PUBLISHED, I have had the
privilege of giving lectures and various presentations on the
life and spirituality of Kahlil Gibran all over the world. I have
been overwhelmed by how many people from every imaginable
culture have been influenced by Gibran's best-known book, *The
Prophet*, which was first published in 1923. Following speaking
engagements, or during book signings, hundreds of people have
shown me their cherished first editions or early publications of *The
Prophet*. As they reverentially handed me the "little black book,"
as it came to be known, they would often explain that it had been
passed down to them by their parents or grandparents and even
great-grandparents, who had themselves been transformed by it,
experiencing it as a sacred text, and that they now keep it in a very
special place in their home, recognizing it as a spiritual treasure.

Many others have shared with me their own personal experience of the impact of *The Prophet* in their own lives. Often
in tears, they have recounted how they were given a copy of
the book during a particularly difficult period in their lives, and
how it profoundly spoke to them, feeding their souls and healing their spirits during times of crises. Others have explained to
me that they attribute *The Prophet* to having literally saved their
lives, as Gibran's words gave them the hope they needed during

times when they were contemplating suicide, enabling them to pull out of the profound depression and hopelessness they were experiencing. For many others, who have been disaffected for whatever reason with institutional religion, *The Prophet* uniquely provided a connection to the Transcendent, feeding their souls' hunger and providing a new spiritual wholeness to their lives. Some have memorized whole sections of *The Prophet* and would recite them for me, saying they hold those words close to their hearts, and recite them when they need spiritual encouragement or inspiration. I have also received hundreds of emails and letters from all over the world, from youth just beginning their life journeys to celebrities, sharing the profound impact Gibran's writings have had on them. It has been a tremendous privilege to hear these moving personal stories of the role *The Prophet* has played in the spiritual journeys of so many people.

At the same time, I have been struck by how little people know, even those who have been profoundly influenced by Gibran's writings, about him, let alone of his life's spiritual journey. This was why I first decided to write this book. After all I have heard and experienced since the publication of this book, I believe more than ever that Gibran can be an unparalleled spiritual guide for our time. Sometimes, something written long ago can become even more relevant than during its own day. Gibran's timeless message, focusing us on an eternal essence, continues to cross cultural and religious divides, East and West, and can speak to readers just as much today as during his lifetime.

Gibran's entire focus was on "awakening" people to their greater selves and to the true heart of God or the Divine. He was confident that his spiritual search was one that would resonate with others. Writing to a relative, he shared, "I know that the principles upon which I base my writings are echoes of the spirit of the great majority of the people of the world, because the tendency towards a spiritual independence is to our life as the heart is to the body."[1]

On the 100ᵗʰ Anniversary of the publication of *The Prophet*, I cannot help but be struck by the prophetic words of Mary Haskell, Gibran's closest friend and benefactress, on October 2, 1923, upon receiving by mail her own copy of the book that Gibran had sent her.

She wrote:

> "This book will be held as one of the treasures of English literature. And in our darkness we will open it to find ourselves again and the heaven and earth within ourselves. Generations will not exhaust it, but instead, generation after generation will find in the book what they would fain be—and it will be better loved as men grow riper and riper. It is the most loving book ever written. . . More will love you as years go by, long long after your body is dust. They will find you in your work. For you are in it as visibly as God is . . . God bless you most dearly, beloved Kahlil, and sing through your mouth more and more of his songs and yours . . ."[2]

Through this book, I invite you to be a companion on Gibran's fascinating journey toward an all-embracing spirituality that so many have resonated with over the last 100 years, and that is more than ever needed in our world today.

—Paul-Gordon Chandler

Introduction

*God has placed in each soul an apostle to lead us upon
the illumined path.
Yet many seek life from without, unaware that it is
within them.*

—KAHLIL GIBRAN, *SPIRITUAL SAYINGS*[1]

I FIRST HEARD OF KAHLIL GIBRAN THROUGH JIHAD, my
friend at boarding school in Côte d'Ivoire. Jihad was a Muslim of the Lebanese diaspora in West Africa. He brought a
little black book titled *The Prophet* back to school after one of our
much-loved holiday breaks and raved about it. Coming from a
Christian family and growing up in the Muslim country of Senegal,
I naturally assumed the book was about Muhammad, the prophet
of Islam, and therefore as a teenager expressed little interest in its
content. Yet I recall being immensely curious as to how this small
book had so captivated my high school friend's attention.

Years later, when just out of university, I remember an American friend being given this same little book for his birthday by his
mother, who introduced its author as a Christian. Having had the
previous experience with Jihad in high school, I found myself cor-
recting her, telling her that the author was instead from a Muslim

1

background. While she had been told otherwise, she believed that I was more of an expert, since I had grown up in a Muslim country, and expressed her gratitude for being set straight, as she didn't really know much about the author either and didn't want to "lead others astray."

That experience immediately began to haunt me, as I knew I had spoken out of a knowledge I did not really have. Who was Kahlil Gibran? While millions have read his most popular book, *The Prophet*, most would be hard-pressed to share much about him. As Alexandre Najjar, one of his contemporary biographers, writes, "He is the most famous stranger on earth, a name without a face, a writer without a legend."[2]

Kahlil Gibran, born Khalil Gibran in 1883 in the mountains of Lebanon, is certainly not easily defined or categorized. His life, writings, and paintings mute distinctions, whether they are religious, literary, or artistic. However, this has not stopped untold numbers of scholars, academics, biographers, religious leaders, New Age gurus, artists, and filmmakers from claiming him as their own, putting their labels on him, or attempting to interpret him through their respective lenses.

Kahlil the poet, Kahlil the novelist, Kahlil the essayist, Kahlil the activist, Kahlil the revolutionary, Kahlil the counterculturist, Kahlil the philosopher, Kahlil the artist, Kahlil the painter, Kahlil the modernizer of Arab literature, Kahlil the prophet, Kahlil the New Age guru, Kahlil the visionary, Kahlil the humanitarian, Kahlil the Sufi, Kahlil the Christian, Kahlil the Universalist, Kahlil the interfaith mentor. . . . Will the real Kahlil please stand up? The renowned contemporary Syrian poet Adonis summed it up perfectly when speaking of Kahlil: "He is a star spinning outside the orbit of that other sun . . . in his universal acceptance."[3]

Kahlil wrote for both the East and the West, presenting a nonsectarian vision of our world and offering his readers a spiritual tapestry that transcends humanity's divisions. And, irrespective of all attempts to understand him, Kahlil remains an enigma. Perhaps this is because essentially everyone, admirers and critics alike, acknowledges he was a mystic who plumbed the depths of the rich spiritual traditions in the Middle East and shared them with the West. The curator of the Soumaya Museum in Mexico City, Héctor Palhares Meza, when discussing Kahlil with me, described him as an "emblematic poet and thinker who put together East and West through his spiritual sensitivity."

Despite the epic success of some of his writings, so much of Kahlil's life and work remains in relative obscurity. How does one begin to approach the spiritual depth of this extraordinary figure, seen as a sage by many, and yet who could have passed as a double for his contemporary, Charlie Chaplin? (Incidentally, this was a comparison that Kahlil himself did not appreciate.) Unlike Chaplin, however, there exists only one segment of film footage of Kahlil, shot toward the end of his life on 16mm and lasting but fifty-four seconds.

Perhaps the best starting point is to acknowledge the overwhelming influence he has had over the last century, both in the East and West. US president Woodrow Wilson purportedly once said to Kahlil, "You are the first Eastern storm to sweep this country, and what a number of flowers it has brought."[4] Kahlil, through his writings and art, has inspired millions worldwide from all walks of life: the rich, the poor, the famous, and the infamous. Referred to by some as a "William Blake [the early eighteenth-century English poet, artist, and mystic] of the twentieth-century," Kahlil had the opportunity of meeting or knowing such luminaries of the early twentieth century as renowned French sculptor Auguste Rodin; Indian Nobel laureate poet Rabindranath Tagore; Irish poet William Butler Yeats; Swiss psychiatrist Carl Jung; prominent American artist Albert P. Ryder; the head of the Baha'i faith, `Abdu'l-Bahá; and the Roosevelt family.

Kahlil's most recognized work, a series of prose poems titled *The Prophet*, has been translated into more than forty languages and has sold more than one hundred million copies, making him one of the most widely read poets in history, behind only Shakespeare and Lao Tzu. Since its first publication in 1923, *The Prophet* has never been out of print, with Kahlil's writings reportedly drawing royalties in excess of one million dollars each year.

While best known for *The Prophet*, Kahlil was also a prolific painter and author of many other works, including extensive correspondence that illuminates his artistic life. His books have been translated into more than one hundred languages, and his drawings and paintings have been exhibited in the capitals of the world. The beauty, cadence, and depth of his writings have been used in innumerable contexts and for myriad purposes. Some have served as alternative sacred texts at baptisms, christenings, weddings, and funerals; others for wooing women.

Many are familiar with the late president John F. Kennedy's exhortation at his 1961 Inaugural Address: "[A]sk not what your country can do for you—ask what you can do for your country." It has become one of the most recognizable statements on civic service. However, most do not know that this statement was adapted from an article Kahlil wrote in Arabic in 1925 titled "The New Frontier," in which he sought to challenge and inspire his own people, the Lebanese.[5]

The influence of Kahlil's life and writings on popular Western culture is manyfold, especially as it relates to the arts. Many music artists have used Kahlil's poetry in their lyrics, including David Bowie, Bob Dylan, the Beatles, and Van Morrison. The once-popular contemporary group Mr. Mister's number-one hit, "Broken Wings," was inspired by Kahlil's book of the same title. Kahlil's work also inspired both Elvis Presley and Johnny Cash.

Those close to Elvis say he gave away thousands of copies of *The Prophet*. Elvis's handwritten notes in his personal copy of the book say, "I will sing his praises for all to hear and spread his message to those I can." It is reported that Elvis once gave a friend a copy of *The Prophet* and said, "Open it up anywhere and read." The friend started reading, and Elvis joined in and finished the page by heart. Shortly before he died, Elvis had ambitious plans to make a film of *The Prophet*.[6]

Elvis's friend and music contemporary Johnny Cash was equally captivated by Kahlil's writings and message. Cash's introduction to Kahlil's work is highlighted in the Oscar-nominated 2005 film *Walk the Line*, starring Joaquin Phoenix and Reese

Witherspoon, when Cash's wife, June Carter, gives him a copy of *The Prophet*.

Cash's passion for Kahlil's writings was caught on tape during a recording session with legendary music producer Rick Rubin for the album *Unearthed*. In the recording, just months before Cash died, he spontaneously shared his thoughts with Rubin on Kahlil and *The Prophet*, which he was being asked to narrate for a recording. Cash's narration of Kahlil's posthumously published *The Eye of the Prophet* is available for purchase today.

Copious screenplays have been written, and plays and films produced, of Kahlil's work, most notably Salma Hayek's production of an animated version of *The Prophet*, directed by Oscar-winning Roger Allers (*The Lion King*). The film's musical score was written by Academy Award–winning composer Gabriel Yared, with music performed by renowned cellist Yo-Yo Ma. Celebrated film stars have portrayed Kahlil in films dispensing his wisdom on the silver screen, such as the legendary late Egyptian actor Omar Sharif. Television resounds with the echoes of Kahlil's work in a multitude of forums, from a *History Detectives* episode about a painting of his, to Hollywood actor Tom Selleck quoting *The Prophet* in the popular American sitcom *Friends*, to a PBS special on how his writings are often used as sacred texts in church ceremonies.

Ironically, Kahlil's popularity grew markedly during the 1960s with the American counterculture, when *The Prophet* became a guidebook during that "free thinking" era. Later, in the 1980s, the spirituality movement adopted him, including the flowering New Age movements.

The global imprint Kahlil made echoes widely. There are memorials to him around the world: in Washington, DC; Boston; Beirut; Yerevan, Armenia; Buenos Aires; Belo Horizonte and Curitiba, Brazil. Numerous streets, parks, schools, and cultural centers are named for him in countries like Canada, France, Romania, Morocco, Venezuela, and Mexico. He has also been the subject of international conferences. The University of Maryland hosts The Kahlil Gibran Chair for Values and Peace, while the

Arab American Institute's top annual honors are called Kahlil Gibran "Spirit of Humanity" Awards. Annually celebrated at a big gala for diplomats and dignitaries, recipients of these awards include former president of Poland Lech Walesa; politicians and diplomats such as John H. Sununu, George Mitchell, Ralph Nader, and Lakhdar Brahimi; journalist Christiane Amanpour; as well as celebrities such as Muhammad Ali, Queen Noor of Jordan, Sting, and Salma Hayek.

Perhaps the most contemporary evidence of the scope of his influence is that Google celebrates his birthday, January 6, in its worldwide daily doodle by replacing the "g" in its logo with a photo of Kahlil Gibran. The words accompanying the doodle are quite telling: "Happy Birthday Gibran Kahlil Gibran. Today marks the birthday of the famous poet, writer and artist. . . . Gibran is a spirit that will never be forgotten, for he has become immortal with the works he left behind." Obviously, Kahlil's timeless message, focusing us on an eternal essence, crosses cultural and religious divides, East and West, and relates to mass audiences even more today than during his lifetime.

This book is not a biography. There are already excellent biographies about Kahlil in print. Rather it is a type of pilgrimage into and through Kahlil's own spiritual journey. It is an exploration into Kahlil's depth of spirituality through his remarkable life and profound works. He shares with our world the eternal verities of all time.

This journey has been an adventure that has taken me all over the world to museums, art galleries, churches and mosques, and through revolutions and counterrevolutions—to Beirut, Boston, Cairo, Paris, New York City, Washington, DC, Detroit, Savannah, and Mexico City. On my expeditions I brought Kahlil along as my companion and guide. Reading his poems and stories in the order he wrote them, in the places he lived and visited, I sought to understand what led him from being someone born into what was then an exclusive and intolerant historic Christian community to becoming one who embraced all in our world, and as a result became one embraced by all.

"A prophet is dead" was one of the headlines in the *New York Sun* on the morning after Kahlil Gibran's death on April 10, 1931.[7]

What kind of "prophet" is he, and what does he have to offer us amid today's global challenges? This is what I set out to discover, taking with me the oft-quoted words of Claude Bragdon, the early-twentieth-century American architect, words he wrote about Kahlil after meeting him. Bragdon sensed that Kahlil's power came from "some great reservoir of spiritual life else it could not have been so universal and so potent, but the majesty and beauty of the language with which he clothed it were all his own."[8]

The Sacred Valley   1

*For in one soul are contained the hopes and feelings of
all Mankind.*

—KAHLIL GIBRAN, *THE VOICE OF THE MASTER*[1]

T HE FLIGHT FROM CAIRO TO BEIRUT is just under an hour.
It was winter, and I was heading to Kahlil's birthplace up
in the Lebanese mountains. At the time I was living in
Cairo working as the rector of the historic Episcopal church serving Egypt's international diplomatic, business, academic, and NGO
(non-governmental organization) communities.

My trip to Beirut was the envy of my American diplomat
friends in Egypt who, due to the US State Department's travel
restrictions, were not permitted to visit Lebanon. Following the
bitter fifteen-year Lebanese civil war that ended in 1990, in the
midst of rebuilding, the country continued to be plagued by political and religious strife. The rise of Hezbollah ("the Party of
God"), the Shia Islamic resistance group whose political party and
paramilitary wing had increasingly exerted their influence over the
country, created an ever-present uneasy tension, a tension that at
times exploded.

Several weeks before my visit, on the picturesque seafront thoroughfare in the predominantly Christian northern section of Beirut,

a car bomb exploded in a US embassy vehicle, killing four and injuring sixteen. The State Department immediately issued a travel advisory: "We strongly advise you to reconsider your need to travel to Lebanon at this time because of the highly volatile security and political situation, which could deteriorate without warning and lead to widespread violence. In these circumstances, departure options may be severely limited. . . . Ongoing tensions could lead to retaliatory or opportunistic bomb attacks against a range of targets. . . . Random shootings continue to occur."

Only a few years earlier, I had arrived in Beirut during what was called the Cedar Revolution, a series of mass demonstrations triggered by the Valentine's Day explosion of eighteen hundred kilograms of TNT in the car bomb assassination of Prime Minister Rafik Hariri. Hariri had been responsible for reconstructing Beirut following the civil war. Most accused Syria of the attack, and Lebanese people of all shades and stripes flocked to the streets to demand the expulsion of the Syrian troops that had been present for almost thirty years. It was an exhilarating moment to see tens of thousands of people from all segments of Lebanese society united. I joined the throng, walking down the streets of Beirut waving the Lebanese flag I'd been given, which proudly displays their national emblem, the Cedar of Lebanon. I particularly remember the moving experience of visiting Rafik Hariri's gravesite (known now as the Hariri Memorial Shrine) near the Mohammad Al-Amin Mosque on the infamous Martyrs' Square in downtown Beirut. In reverent silence, amid the scent of thousands of lit candles, hundreds of Christians, Muslims, and Druze lined up in a spirit of oneness paying homage to this man whose death had inspired them toward a new hope and freedom.

I was in Beirut at that time conducting interviews and doing research for a book on the Syrian novelist Mazhar Mallouhi. As someone who calls himself a Sufi Muslim follower of Christ, Mazhar's life and writings have uniquely served to bridge the chasm of misunderstanding between Muslims and Christians throughout the Arab world. Regrettably, the atmosphere of hope and goodwill in the air during that visit did not last long. Hariri's assassination marked the beginning of a series of assassinations that resulted in the death of many prominent Lebanese figures. Mazhar himself, just prior to my arrival, had been near the explosion of a huge car bomb, which ended in a spontaneous firefight, killing six.

On this visit Mazhar had graciously offered to host me and to drive me up to Kahlil Gibran's hometown village. I arrived at Rafik Hariri International Airport, again noticing how relaxed security seemed in contrast to when Syria had been the shadow government there. However, one is always cautious to never have an Israeli entry stamp in one's passport, since Lebanon is officially at war with Israel. Handing my passport to the immigration official, I watched him flip carefully through it page by page, searching for Israeli stamps. As I exited the airport, Mazhar was eagerly waiting for me, Muslim prayer beads in hand. In typical Lebanese style, expressing the warmth of his welcome, we headed straight to indulge in Lebanon's renowned cuisine, which he duly informed me was awaiting us in a magnificent restaurant operated by Hezbollah in South Beirut.

The streets were lined the entire way with hundreds of posters, banners, and billboards of the stern, bearded face of Imad Mughniyah, the most wanted Lebanese Hezbollah terrorist, who had been assassinated by a car bomb while hiding in Damascus a few days earlier. Known as "The Fox," Mughniyah had been hunted for more than twenty years by the world's most powerful intelligence agencies for his alleged role in numerous bombings, kidnappings, and hijackings, most notably the hijacking of TWA Flight 847 in 1985. With a bounty of five million dollars on his head, he had eluded all attempts by operatives to capture or assassinate him until now. His funeral in Beirut had been held just a few days before my arrival, during which Hezbollah's leader-in-hiding, Hassan Nasrallah, promised retaliation. Mughniyah, now seen as a martyr, was being hailed throughout southern Lebanon as a hero. It was a tense moment in Lebanon.

At the Hezbollah restaurant, Mazhar, in introducing me to his friends, the Shia Muslim owners, explained that I had come to

Lebanon to work on a book about Kahlil Gibran. Immediately they expressed their enthusiasm for what I was doing and their overwhelming love of Kahlil and his writings. They went on to share one of Kahlil's short stories that was popular in their youth and told of their intentions to pass it on to their children.

Where is Kahlil Gibran in this modern-day Lebanon, this country that he loved so passionately and that so inspired him spiritually until the end of his life? In 1920, years after having immigrated to the United States, Kahlil expressed his love for Lebanon with these prophetic words:

> You have your Lebanon and I have mine. You have your Lebanon with her problems, and I have my Lebanon with her beauty. You have your Lebanon with all her prejudices and struggles, and I have my Lebanon with all her dreams and securities. Your Lebanon is a political knot, a national dilemma, a place of conflict and deception. My Lebanon is a place of beauty and dreams of enchanting valleys and splendid mountains. Your Lebanon is inhabited by functionaries, officers, politicians, committees, and factions. My Lebanon is for peasants, shepherds, young boys and girls, parents and poets. Your Lebanon is empty and fleeting, whereas My Lebanon will endure forever.[2]

Kahlil's Lebanon. This is what I had set out to discover. My starting point would be the small Christian village of Bsharri, high in the snowy mountains near the great cedar forests, Kahlil's birthplace and the location of the Kahlil Gibran Museum, his final resting place.

A severe snowstorm had unexpectedly swept across the mountains overnight, breaking records and creating hazardous conditions as snow levels rose. Our journey up into the region would be precarious to say the least. The blizzard was steadily escalating as we

drove, and the elemental blasts of pure winter winds made nego-
tiating icy roads and sharp bends hugging plunging cliff drop-offs a
sheer matter of faith. Twice we had to stop and dig ourselves out
of deep snowdrifts. However, despite the frigid cold, the military
checkpoints were in full operation. Soldiers diligently stopped our
car and asked about our destination while taking furtive glances
into our backseat. As our passports were being checked, I noticed
a frozen waterfall, stopped in midflow, tumbling down toward
the sea.

As we climbed along the edges of winding mountain roads, we
drove past dozens of posters displaying a photograph of someone
who looked very much like Kahlil. But it was not Kahlil. These
were political posters of Samir Geagea, a Christian politician and
leader of the Lebanese Forces. A controversial figure during the
Lebanese Civil War, he was eventually convicted in 1994 for
ordering various political assassinations and was imprisoned, held
in solitary confinement for eleven years, before being granted am-
nesty in the wake of the Cedar Revolution in 2005. He grew up
in the cedar forest region, as did Kahlil some eighty years earlier,
and the resemblance was so striking that I thought they could have
been brothers.

Finally the road signs indicated we were in the Bsharri District
of North Lebanon, five thousand feet above sea level. We passed
through the mountainous village of Dimane and by the beautiful
garden of the summer residence of the patriarch of the Maronite
Catholic Church.

There were crosses everywhere: along the streets, on steep
hillsides, on the mountaintops, and painted on houses. This was
Maronite land, the heart of the Christian community in Lebanon.

The Maronites are an ancient church that traces its origins as
far back as the fifth century AD, when the early Christians of Syria
pledged their allegiance to a legendary monk, St. Maroun. Despite
an allegiance with the Church of Rome, the Maronites preserve
their ancient Eastern Syriac liturgy and the right of their priests to
marry. Toughened from centuries of invasions and occupations,
the Maronites are fiercely protective of their land and culture.

They were brought to the world's attention during the Lebanese civil war through the fighting of the various Maronite militias, most notably the feared Phalangists.

Passing by the patriarch's garden, I was reminded of a photograph I have in my office, taken in the early 1900s. It is of a rotund Maronite patriarch, sitting in his rocking chair out in a garden dressed in all his ecclesiastical regalia, fast asleep. Regrettably, the peaceful image of the sleeping patriarch does not accurately reflect the tensions that exist in Lebanon's deeply sectarian society. Yet life goes on, in the midst of conflict, war, and peace. I recall an image from a visit to Beirut's "Green Line," that infamous divide during the civil war separating Muslim West Beirut from Christian East Beirut. Just a year after the truce was reached, amid shelled-out buildings and rubble, I saw two elderly men sitting on plastic chairs leaning over a rickety table playing backgammon, as though nothing else in the world mattered.

We continued the treacherous drive up the snowy roads, hugging the edge of the famous Qadisha Valley, known in Arabic as Wadi Qadisha, meaning "The Sacred Valley." This deep gorge has sheltered Christian communities for many centuries. Looking out across the valley, we could see the ancient footpaths leading from the village's parish church down to the bottom of the valley where the Maronites, often led by their patriarch, took refuge after the Arab Muslim invasions in the seventh century. The Lebanese writer Marun Abbud gives voice to the region:

> All the peoples of the earth have passed through this land. They fought battles and then departed, leaving behind traces of their cultural heritage, which combine to form the fabric of our way of thinking. There is no other nation on earth that can claim such an interlacing of thoughts. . . . In Lebanon you can find convents and temples, fortresses and citadels, churches, cathedrals, mosques, amphitheaters, and stadiums. On each peak stands a convent, on each hill you can find a temple or a fortress, and in each valley a fortified refuge.[3]

While for the Maronites the "sacredness" of the valley has been inherently linked to the security it has provided over the centuries, to a visitor the magnificent and breathtaking views across the valley alone seem reason enough to justify its descriptive name. As we rounded the bend, I found myself totally unprepared for the scene that was to greet me. On the opposite side of the Sacred Valley, majestically perched below towering Mount Lebanon, sat the breathtakingly beautiful village of Bsharri. Blanketed in freshly fallen snow, the village was postcard-like, resting next to the great cedar forests of biblical renown. Balanced five thousand feet up on a narrow ridge between the edge of the Sacred Valley's deep gorges and steep mountains, a spectacular church rose up out of the heart of the village. Its bells melodiously welcomed us, breaking through the muffled silence of the cold winter's day.

Several feet of deep snow blocked the last quarter-mile of the road leading to the Gibran Museum, so I completed the journey by foot. At the top of the road I was greeted by a large ethereal sculpture of Kahlil, only partially carved out of the rock, emerging as if to say that he and this land were one. There was an innately spiritual atmosphere to the place.

During Kahlil's childhood the museum was the Mar Sarkis (St. Sergius) Carmelite Hermitage, and he played throughout its grounds. Today it is a hermitage of a different sort, and the grotto is Kahlil's final resting place, as requested in his will. The museum holds an extensive collection of his paintings, writings, letters, and many of his personal belongings: his library, furniture, and much of the art he collected.

On this day, because of the perilous road conditions, I was the only visitor. But from the sensations this place evoked, I fully understood how it attracted more than fifty thousand visitors a year. Standing outside the museum's entrance, looking over the Sacred Valley, I heard the mystical melodies of the *nay* (Middle Eastern flute) echoing from the museum out into the garden. On a nearby hill I watched a young boy jumping around in the snow with his friends. The icy wind of winter seemed to be holding its breath, listening to the joyful shouts of the playing children.

While Kahlil was here more than a century ago, it was not so difficult to enter into his world; so little had changed. I was carried to a time when the world may have seemed less complicated. This storied setting formed the foundation of Kahlil's lifelong search for spiritual depth, which was beautifully translated into his outpouring of art and writing.

※

At the dawn of a new year, during the heart of winter and high in this mountain village, Kahlil was born into a Maronite Catholic family on Eastern Christmas Day, January 6, 1883. Bsharri was then a semi-autonomous part of the Ottoman Empire and referred to as Syria. His mother, Kamila, was the daughter of a priest and his father, Khalil, was her second husband. Kahlil's father initially worked in an apothecary, but prone to drink and with gambling debts rising, he went to work for a local Ottoman-appointed administrator. Around 1891 the administrator was removed and his staff investigated. Kahlil's father was imprisoned for embezzlement, and the family's property was confiscated. While his father was eventually released, Kahlil's mother resolved to follow other relatives and begin a new life in North America, as many Lebanese were doing at the time. Kahlil and his mother, together with his three siblings, Peter, Marianna, and Sultana, left Lebanon in 1895. Although Kahlil spent only twelve short years in this magical setting, it was to serve as the foundation of his spirituality and worldview for the rest of his life.

Kahlil was a retiring and pensive child. Recognizing his need for solitude, his mother helped facilitate this for him. Later in life he recalled, "[S]ometimes she would smile at someone who came in . . . and lay her finger on her lips and say, 'Hush. He's not here.'" He was also innately creative and at an early age would draw and sculpt objects. When he was alone he would draw with a pencil, if he had one, or with a piece of charcoal, on paper or stones. Observing her son's artistic inclination, his mother gave him a book of Leonardo da Vinci's collected works. For Kahlil it was a profound revelation. In admiration of the great power of the Italian painter, he later reflected, "I never got over the feeling somewhere in the recesses of my soul that part of his spirit was lodged in my own. I was a child when I saw the drawings of this amazing man for the first time. I will never forget that moment as long as I live. It was as if a ship lost in the fog had suddenly found a compass."[4]

Naturally inquisitive and imaginative, Kahlil loved to build toys and kites and to collect things, with a particular love for stones. The story is told of how, at the age of four, he planted bits of paper in his garden and waited patiently for a harvest full of paper leaves. Together with his half-brother and two younger sisters he intermittently attended a one-room school led by a visiting priest, learning the elementary basics of Arabic, Syriac, and math.

The strongest influence on Kahlil was undoubtedly the splendor of nature all around him—the valleys, waterfalls, rivers, rugged cliffs, cedars, and mountains—which absorbed him fully. He was known to escape into the hidden monasteries in the deep gorges of the Sacred Valley, finding needed solace in the wonder of nature. Profoundly moved by these symbols of God's love and the wonders of the natural world, he recalled much later his early impressions:

> The first great moment that I remember was when I was three years old—a storm—I tore my clothes and ran out in it. Do you remember when you first saw the sea? I was eight. My mother was on a horse, and my father and I were on a beautiful large Cyprian donkey, white. We rode up the mountain pass, and as we came over the ridge, the sea was before us. The sea and the sky were of one color. There was no horizon and the water was full of the large Eastern sailing vessels with sails all set. As we passed across the mountains, suddenly I saw what looked like an immeasurable heaven and the ships sailing in it.
>
> I remember when I was taken to the ruins of Baalbek—the most wonderful ruins in the world. I was about nine then—my

father was on a horse, and my mother was on another. I was on a pony, and our two men on mules. We stayed about four days at Baalbek—and when we left I wept. I have a notebook of the sketches I made there.[5]

All his life Kahlil drew inspiration from the majestic beauty of that enchanted setting and was filled with nostalgia for his homeland. His writings would celebrate the dignity and freedom of animals, birds, the seasons, oceans, and clouds. The scenery, and power of its ancient lore, became a part of his being. As Kahlil once wrote to his cousin:

The things which the child loves remains in the domain of the heart until old age. The most beautiful thing in life is that our souls remain hovering over the places where we once enjoyed ourselves. I am one of those who remember those places regardless of time and place.[6]

Years later, in reflecting on the beauty of his sense of oneness with all of God's creation, Kahlil wrote:

You work that you may keep pace with the earth and the soul of the earth. For to be idle is to become a stranger unto the seasons, and to step out of life's procession, that marches in majesty and proud submission towards the infinite.[7]

In contrast to his peaceful surroundings, Kahlil was born into a period of political and interreligious strife, as well as corruption by religious authorities, during the later part of a four-hundred-year-long Ottoman occupation. Prior to disputes that led to the massacres beginning in 1860, the intermingling of religions was typical of Christians and Muslims in the nineteenth century. The story told of his maternal grandfather's origins provides a glimpse into this interaction. Two Muslim horsemen were said to have entered Bsharri one day and, liking what they found, converted to Christianity, abandoning their Islamic faith, settling in the town, and marrying into his mother's clan.[8] Although childhood friends from his village were of Christian background, Kahlil enjoyed Muslim friends in the summers when they left Bsharri to visit the farm his father owned, not far from the ruins of ancient Baalbek farther east.

Thanks to his mother, Kahlil was taught the biblical stories, which captured his imagination at a young age. In her company, he went to church every Sunday, attended Mass, and tried to learn the liturgy in Syriac.[9] His friend Mikhail (Mischa) Naimy recounted that on one Good Friday, Kahlil was found at the village cemetery with a bouquet of cyclamen flowers in his hands. He was too young to go with the other village children to gather flowers to place at the crucifix in church during the Mass. Left to his own devices, he mysteriously disappeared, causing his parents much anguish. Kahlil later explained to his mother that when he arrived at church to place the flowers, which he had himself picked, he found the gate closed, so he went to the cemetery to look for Christ's tomb.[10]

Later in life Kahlil recalled an impacting event that occurred shortly before the family sailed for America:

> When I was ten or eleven years old, I was in a monastery one day with another boy, a cousin, a little older. We were walking along a very high place that fell off more than a thousand feet. . . . The path had a handrail, but it had weakened—and path and rail and all fell with us—and we rolled probably one hundred and fifty yards in the landslide. My cousin fractured his leg, and I got several wounds and cuts in the head down to the skull, and injured my shoulder. The shoulder healed crooked—too high and too far forward. So they pulled it apart again and strapped me to a real cross with thirty yards of strap and I stayed wrapped to that cross forty days. I slept and all sitting up. I was not strong enough to take ether when they broke the shoulder again. If it had hurt less, I should probably have cried out. But it hurt too much for me to cry. My father and mother were with me talking to me.[11]

Even as a child Kahlil drew from strong reservoirs and processed this childhood trauma through the symbolism of biblical imagery. His splint became a cross, and he languished in pain for the same period Christ spent in the wilderness.

Throughout his life Kahlil's writings would resound with biblical imagery. His familiarity with the Bible became a bridge in his writings between East and West. These early religious experiences became the wellspring that watered his inspiration and from which the language of his soul flowed forth.

Influences from Kahlil's childhood spent in the Sacred Valley resound throughout his first published book, appropriately titled *Nymphs of the Valley*. Published in 1906, it is a collection of three short stories originally written in Arabic for an audience of Arab immigrants in America. His fresh approach to storytelling—the sardonic tone, the anticlerical critique, a focus on peasants and those from the working class—was markedly different from the formal classical Arabic style and genre of his day. And his work immediately appealed to the émigré writers in America.[12]

One of the stories in *Nymphs of the Valley* is titled "Yuhanna the Mad." Kahlil had only just emerged from his adolescent years and gives us at the outset of his writing career a glimpse of the wealth and depth of spirit he was drawing from, both from his own childhood and from the natural bent of his contemplative personality. The roots of Kahlil's own childhood infuse this tale with life. He crafted this story around the life of a child, a quiet simple shepherd boy who lives in the rugged hills of Lebanon. We see themes emerging that he will explore for a lifetime: his innate bond with nature and the cycle of its seasons, his fascination with the person of Jesus in the Gospels versus Jesus of the "Christian," and appreciation for an empathetic mother who understood him and guarded his soul with her own.

The story opens:

> And in the summer Yuhanna went out every morning to the field leading his oxen and his calves and carrying his plough over his shoulder, the while listening to the songs of the thrushes and the rustling of the leaves in the trees. At noontide he sat beside the dancing stream that wound its way through the lowland of the green meadows, where he ate his food, leaving unfinished morsels of bread on the grass for the birds. In the evening, when the setting sun took with it the light of day, he returned to his

humble dwelling, which looked out over the villages and hamlets of North Lebanon.[13]

Although written years after immigrating to America, Kahlil gleans inspiration from these rich images of life in the setting of his childhood home.

During long winter nights Yuhanna

> would open a wooden chest and take out of it the book of the Gospels to read from it in secret by the feeble glow of a lamp, looking stealthily from time to time in the direction of his slumbering father, who had forbidden him to read the Book. It was forbidden because the priests did not allow the simple in mind to probe the secrets of the teachings of Jesus. If they did so, then the church would excommunicate them. Thus did Yuhanna pass the days of his youth between that field of wonder and beauty and the book of Jesus, filled with the light and the spirit.[14]
>
> Whenever he went to church he returned with a feeling of sorrow because the teachings that he heard from the pulpit and altar were not those that he read about in the Gospel. And the life led by the faithful and their leaders was not the beautiful life of which Jesus of Nazareth spoke in His book.[15]

Kahlil's admiration of Jesus of Nazareth, in contrast to what he saw as Jesus of the "Christian," became a lifelong passion, culminating several decades later in his book *Jesus the Son of Man*. He rejected the hypocrisy of what he must have observed at some level as a child, and although he did not adhere to the traditional religion of his forefathers, he chose to embrace the divine essence in all and became a lifelong pilgrim toward the depths of spirituality.

Eventually Yuhanna finds spring in the air, and the symbolic theme of a river makes its debut, an image that Kahlil repeatedly turned to throughout his life and revisited in many of his future writings:

> On the mountaintops some snow still remained until it in turn melted and ran down the mountainsides and became streams

twisting and winding in the valleys below. Soon they met and joined one another until they were swift-flowing rivers, their roaring announcing to all that Nature had awakened from her sleep.[16]

One day toward the end of Lent, Yuhanna

carried his Bible under his cloak so that nobody should see it, until he reached the meadow that rested on the shoulder of the valley near the fields of a monastery which stood up grimly like a tower in the midst of the hillocks. There his calves dispersed to pasture on the grass. Yuhanna sat . . . down against a rock, now looking across the valley in all its beauty, now reading the words in his book that spoke to him of the Kingdom of Heaven.[17]

The negative foreshadowing of the looming monastery soon gives way to a dramatic tale. Young Yuhanna's calves mistakenly wander into the gardens of the monastery and a sad series of events unfold, in which self-righteous monks berate him and threaten him with insurmountable fines, heedless of his pleas for mercy. The boy musters the courage to question their hypocrisy, as they in turn attempt to discredit him with claims of insanity. Only his mother believes in him and comes to his rescue, as the story powerfully unfolds with writing full of symbolism, echoing the sufferings of Christ and exploring deep questions at the heart of life.

※

The early years Kahlil spent exploring the Sacred Valley of his childhood were especially formative ones. As he grew into young adulthood, the fruits of those experiences began to take shape and search for creative ways of expression. His natural gifts in both art and writing emerged as opportunities to give voice to his inner journey, already deeply spiritual.

On my return flight to Cairo I sat next to a middle-aged man who asked why I had been to Lebanon. When I shared about my visit to Kahlil Gibran's birthplace, he went on to share with me how as a child he had learned Kahlil's poetry through the songs of Fayrouz, the most widely admired and respected living singer in the Arab world. From Lebanon, her songs are heard throughout the Middle East. She sings about Lebanon—the beauty of its mountains, snow, and sun, and the indomitable free spirit of its people. Also of Maronite Christian background, Fayrouz frequently uses Kahlil's poetry in her lyrics. My seat companion began to spontaneously hum the tune of one of Fayrouz's most popular songs of Kahlil's poetry. Then he began singing the words in Arabic for me. When those sitting on the other side of the aisle heard him singing it, they spontaneously joined in. Soon the row in front of me and the one behind me were also enthusiastically singing the song, which now surreally and joyously echoed these words through the cabin:

> Bring me the flute and sing, for song is the secret to
>   eternity. . .
> Have you taken the forest, rather than the palace, to be
>   your home?
> Have you climbed up the creeks and the rocks?
> Have you sat alone at dusk among the grapevines?
> Among their clusters hanging like chandeliers of gold?
> Have you made the grass your night-time bed?
> Have you wrapped yourself in the evening air with the
>   sky for a blanket?[18]

I think Kahlil would have been pleased, for his first piece of published writing was about music, written when he was just twenty-two years old and longing for the Sacred Valley of his childhood. In this essay titled "Music" (*Al Musiqah*), he wrote these lyrical words:

> I sat by one whom my heart loves, and I listened to her
>   words.
> My soul began to wander in the infinite spaces where the
> universe appeared like a dream . . .
> This is Music, oh friends . . .
> My friends: Music is the language of spirits. Its melody is
>   like
> the frolicsome breeze that makes the strings quiver with
> love. When the gentle fingers of Music knock at the door
> of our feelings, they awaken memories that have long lain
> hidden in the depths of the Past. The sad strains of Music
> bring us mournful recollections; and her quiet strains
>   bring
> us joyful memories. The sound of strings makes us weep at
> the departure of a dear one, or makes us smile at the
>   peace
> God has bestowed upon us.
> The soul of Music is of the Spirit, and her mind is of the
> Heart.
> Our souls are like tender flowers at the mercy of the
>   winds of
> Destiny. They tremble in the morning breeze, and bend
> their heads under the falling dews of heaven.
> The song of the bird awakens Man from his slumber and
> invites him to join in the psalms of glory to Eternal
> Wisdom that has created the song of the bird.
> Such music makes us ask ourselves the meaning of the
>   mysteries
> contained in ancient books.[19]

The Heretic

2

*We are all prisoners but some of us are in cells
with windows and some without.*

—KAHLIL GIBRAN, SAND AND FOAM[1]

NO, SIR, WE DON'T KNOW HIM. HE IS NOT HERE. We do not know him. He is not here, sir." The man in the Great Taste Chinese Bakery & Restaurant at 61 Beach Street in South Boston was clearly uncomfortable with my questions. I had asked him if he knew that this was the location where Kahlil Gibran's family had once had a shop. Immediately a sense of tension and unease rippled throughout the restaurant. I was visiting Boston and all the places associated with Kahlil's early life in America. However, my prodding questions about someone they had never heard of greatly alarmed the Chinese in the restaurant, perhaps suspecting I was an immigration official. Not wanting to cause more discomfort, I thanked them kindly and stepped back into Boston's modern-day Chinatown.

The life of an immigrant can be deeply unsettling. Far from the familiar sights and sounds of their home country, they are plunged into an alien setting: a language they don't speak fluently and a culture that seems so strange, loaded with social nuances they cannot

understand. Upon reaching the shores of America, Kahlil and his
family found themselves facing a tremendously vulnerable transi-
tion. Ironically, well over a century later, the situation in Boston's
South End does not seem to have changed that much.

In 1895, at the age of twelve, Kahlil, along with his mother
and three siblings, set off on an arduous journey through the
Mediterranean Sea, across the Atlantic Ocean to Ellis Island in
New York, where they were processed through Immigration.
They eventually settled near relatives in Boston's South End, then
the second-largest Syrian-Lebanese American community in the
United States after New York. This area of Boston, then popu-
lated with half a million people, remains an immigrant area, home
to the city's East Asian community. Kahlil's mother began selling
lace and linens door to door to Boston's middle and upper class,
peddling, as was common among the Arab immigrant community
then. Eventually she was able to work in the more settled role of
a seamstress. Her income enabled Kahlil's older brother Peter to
set up a goods shop to help support the family.

The long journey from Bsharri to Boston was much more than
geographical. It must have been profoundly disorienting for the
young Kahlil, having been uprooted from the rural beauty of the
Lebanese mountains and thrust into the heart of late-nineteenth-
century poverty-stricken industrialization in a strange and distant
land whose language he did not know. At the same time, being
an Arab immigrant in this new world served to shape his distinct
identity, an identity that would later enable him to artistically and
spiritually bridge the worlds of East and West.

The most renowned contemporary Arab writer today is the
Lebanese-French novelist Amin Maalouf, who has achieved literary global renown, winning the Prix Goncourt, an appointment
to the prestigious Académie française, and nomination for the
Nobel Prize for Literature. As an Arab who writes from France,
Maalouf's work very much embodies the spirit of Kahlil, his fellow countryman. Having immigrated to France during the Lebanese civil war, Maalouf has a foot in both worlds, enabling him a
two-faced Janus view of identity. In Maalouf's excellent book *In*

the Name of Identity, he is expressively descriptive of the unique identity Kahlil would soon embody. Maalouf concludes there is no permanent, monolithic identity, but a series of what he calls "allegiances": history, customs, religion, gender, class, and the worldviews they involve. Maalouf argues that the individual is the sum of all their surroundings, and that it is from this complexity that we build ourselves and are built.

Maalouf writes, "What makes me myself rather than anyone else is the very fact that I am poised between two countries, two or three languages, and several cultural traditions. It is precisely this that defines my identity. . . . Every individual is a meeting ground for many different allegiances."[2] Maalouf's definition pointedly echoes the person Kahlil became. Years later, Mary Haskell, who became his patron, described in her diary the personal dichotomy that Kahlil felt all his life: "He lives in two worlds—Syria and America—and is at home in neither."[3]

Kahlil started learning English in a special class at a school for immigrants, where his name was simplified in English for pronunciation purposes from his given name in Lebanon, Gibran Khalil Gibran, to Kahlil Gibran. At school he showed particular promise in his classes of drawing and painting, and as a result was able to enroll in an art class for immigrant children at a settlement center known as Denison House.

Through his teachers, Kahlil was introduced to the Bostonian artist Fred Holland Day, an avant-garde photographer and publisher, who encouraged his creativity and introduced him to the vast world of literature, even using some of Kahlil's drawings as book covers. Day was profoundly influential, intellectually and artistically, and opened up Kahlil's cultural world. Kahlil's association with Day introduced him to the world of art and literature, as well as to artists and art patrons in Boston's establishment, such as Sarah Choate Sears, the close friend of both artist Mary Cassatt and art collector Gertrude Stein.

A countercultural progressive, Day not only was known to push the artistic norm in the new art form of photography but also published forward-leaning literature like Oscar Wilde's *Salome*, the distinguished British literary periodical *The Yellow Book*, and Stephen Crane's poetry collection, *Black Riders*. Day introduced his eager pupil to much of the literature of Romantic poets and their Symbolist successors.

Echoes of transcendentalism still reverberated in New England through poets like Louise Guiney, Lilla Cabot Perry, and Josephine Peabody, focusing on the mystical dimension of our existence and the wonder of nature. Kahlil's naturally mystical bent found this world highly appealing. And it was through Day that Kahlil discovered *The Treasure of the Humble* by Belgian Symbolist writer Maurice Maeterlinck. It was to be a book of spiritual awakening for Kahlil during his formative teenage years, a book of reflective mystical essays, speaking of the oneness of the individual with the Absolute.

As Kahlil's mother and older brother watched him absorb these Western influences, they became concerned that he was losing too much of his Arab culture and values. Their solution was to send him back to Lebanon at age fifteen to complete his high school studies at a Maronite Catholic boarding school in Beirut.

It was a gorgeous day in Beirut. The sky was wondrously clear, something that was very rare in Cairo, where I had been living. The fresh smell of the sea filled the air as I drove to visit the Gibran Khalil Gibran Garden, on the way to East Beirut, where Kahlil had spent his high school years.

The Gibran Garden is not easily reached and is hidden down below the Central Beirut Ring Road, Fouad Chehab Avenue, an overpass thoroughfare that goes through the heart of the city. Two blocks away sits the shelled-out Beirut City Center cinema, known at "The Egg," an icon of the Lebanese civil war. In spite of its chaotic location, there was a special tranquility to the garden.

It encompasses more than an acre of green grass directly in front of the United Nations House, the headquarters of the UN Economic and Social Commission for Western Asia (ESCWA). The exquisite garden features two circular lawns, six obelisks, a fountain, a modern art sculpture, and a large bust of Kahlil at one end.

Due to its central location in front of the UN building, the Gibran Garden is often used as a venue for peaceful and democratic demonstrations and sit-ins. The day I visited was no exception. I parked next to rusted barbed wire, edging the side of the garden that had undoubtedly been used for recent protests. Positioned front and center were two elderly women sitting outside tents. As I approached I noticed dozens of photographs of young men and women attached to the fence dividing the garden from the UN building. My curiosity aroused, I asked the women about the photos and learned that they were pictures of those who had disappeared during the civil war and were still suspected of being held in Syria. The women explained that they were part of a protest movement called SOLDE (Support of Lebanese in Detention and Exile). Then they went on to tell their personal stories, stories of heartache and separation. One elderly mother cried as she told of the disappearance of her twenty-three-year-old daughter more than twenty years ago. The other held up a photograph of her son, who had disappeared a few years before that; five years ago she learned he was still being held in a Syrian prison. Due to all the political complications between Lebanon and Syria, their children had all but been forgotten. They were determined to keep protesting until someone listened to their plight.

As a teenager just learning his way in a "new world," Kahlil suddenly found himself back in Beirut, many thousands of miles away from his mother, the only person to date who seemed to really understand him. The sense of longing for his family—as a child being sent off to boarding school for the first time to the other side of the world—must have been profound. They had arranged for him to attend a prominent Maronite Catholic School in the Achrafieh district of East Beirut, the Collège de la Sagesse

(College of Wisdom), with the hope that their revered Middle Eastern values would be instilled into him anew during this formative stage in his life.

≬

My lunch in Achrafieh, East Beirut, was at the chic Frida restaurant, named for Mexican artist Frida Kahlo. I was meeting with Nadine Labaki, the renowned Lebanese actor and movie director, whose recent film *Where Do We Go Now?* garnered global attention, premiering at the Cannes Film Festival and winning the People's Choice Award at the Toronto International Film Festival. The film humorously and poignantly addresses the religious tensions between Christians and Muslims and how critical it is that they live together peacefully. This was a message Kahlil intensely absorbed while studying in Beirut as a young man and that is reflected in his writings throughout his life. Also dining with us was the film producer of Kahlil's *The Prophet*, so our conversation naturally gravitated to discussing Kahlil's continuing legacy in Lebanon. "To this day, there is no one who more poetically illustrates for Lebanese the importance of coexistence, and seeing the beauty in each other's traditions, than Kahlil Gibran," remarked Nadine, as we reflected on how he went to high school just around the corner.

The Collège de la Sagesse, located on a hill, is in one of the oldest districts of East Beirut.

Today, Achrafieh is both a residential and a commercial district, with narrow winding streets and luxurious apartment and office buildings. However, during Kahlil's high school years, Achrafieh was mostly farmland owned by a few Greek Orthodox Christian families that had ruled the country and the region for centuries and were considered Beirut's *"haute société."* During Lebanon's civil war, which started in 1975, bombs and rockets wiped out a significant part of Achrafieh's architectural heritage. The area became a major strategic base for the Christian militias led by Bachir Gemayel, and as such formed part of Christian East Beirut. Walking around the neighborhood today, it is evident that the destruction of old buildings continues in order to construct tall modern structures that overshadow the few remaining historic neighborhoods.

Kahlil thrived in his studies at the Collège de la Sagesse, being allowed to follow a special curriculum focused on Arabic and French and their literature, as well as art, religion, and ethics. One of the priests in charge of the school was purportedly struck by Kahlil's self-understanding, which led to his being allowed to pursue a more personalized approach to his studies. During his first meeting with the senior teacher, Father Yusef Haddad, Kahlil told him he wanted to focus on Arabic language and its literature, and not be "relegated" to an elementary class. When the priest explained that learning was like climbing a ladder, one rung at a time, Kahlil's subsequent response took the priest by surprise, impressing him: "Does not the teacher know that the bird does not ascend a ladder in its flight?"[4]

While in Beirut, Kahlil started a literary magazine with a classmate and won the school's poetry award. His summers were spent with his father back in the village of his birth, Bsharri, but sadly his father could not understand his creative side, causing much rejection and suffering for Kahlil. During those two and a half years, he fell under the spell of love twice, but each ended in great pain. One relationship was shut down by an older brother (Hala); the other was lost to death (Sultana).

I arrived at 78 Tyler Street in Boston's South End and looked up at the redbrick building before me. After I rang the doorbell several times, a Chinese priest slowly opened the heavy, arched wooden door. With a faint hesitancy he bowed slightly, unclear as to the reason for my visit. Learning that I was aware that this was the site of the former Maronite Catholic Church, he enthusiastically showed me their little chapel. During Kahlil's time it was the local parish church for the immigrant Lebanese Maronite Catholic community, known as Our Lady of the Cedars. It was just a few blocks from his tenement apartment and a few doors down from the old Quincy School he attended as a young boy, which still functions as an educational center today. Interestingly, while the Maronite Church of Kahlil's day burned down in 1959, the rebuilt building is still a Catholic church today, albeit now the Chinese Catholic Pastoral Center.

As I sat quietly by myself in the chapel imagining the child Kahlil sitting in church with his mother, brother, and sisters for weekly masses, I found myself wondering whether he ever entered this church for assistance after the tremendous losses he experienced upon his return to Boston after his schooling in Lebanon. When tragedy struck, did Kahlil seek the aid of Father Yazbek, the young and energetic Lebanese priest of his local parish?

In 1902 Kahlil made his way back to Boston via Paris, and while there he learned that his fourteen-year-old sister Sultana had just died of tuberculosis. The following year his brother died of tuberculosis as well, and then his mother died of cancer. With these devastating circumstances to deal with emotionally, after working to settle the debts of the family's store, Kahlil poured himself into his painting. His sister Marianna worked at a dressmaker's shop in order to help support them both. In 1904 Day's Harcourt Studios hosted Kahlil's first art exhibition, during which he met Mary Haskell, the headmistress of Boston's Marlborough Street School for Girls, who became his lifelong benefactor, advisor, and guiding spirit. Unbeknownst to him at the time, several years later Mary would sponsor him to study art in Paris for two years, an experience that would deeply influence his life's work.

As if Kahlil had not experienced enough loss, one day his entire collection of artwork was burned in a fire at Day's studio. For Kahlil, this was a devastating series of losses, and in the next few years, perhaps searching for consolation, he began to throw himself deeply into the world of Arab émigré writers. He began contributing articles and essays to Arab-American newspapers, publishing books for an Arabic-language imprint, and helping to organize the Golden Links, a group of Arab-Americans in Boston who met regularly for discussions and lectures.

During this time his emerging prophetic voice was maturing with conviction and confidence. As an immigrant, he discovered he had the liberty to write in a way that he would not have been able to while living in the Arab world. The avoidance of shame in Middle Eastern culture is paramount. In a shame-based culture, appearance is everything. All is done to preserve honor, whether it be for an individual, a family, or a community. Writers and artists often practice self-censorship to avoid governmental or religious oppression, which brings humiliation upon the family. Having lived and worked in the region for many years, I know of numerous examples of artist-activists speaking out against authoritarian regimes, only then to hear that dreaded knock on the door at night and disappear, their whereabouts remaining unknown. Perhaps due to having lived in Lebanon again during his later teenage years, Kahlil realized upon his return to America that he could write with greater boldness without repercussions. Hence his stories and articles began to daringly address highly sensitive issues.

Kahlil's writing began to call on his Lebanese people to question ideologies as he himself began to grapple with religion and spirituality. Throughout his life, Kahlil had a tenuous relationship with the Church, and early on he was deeply disturbed by his observations of oppressive leadership in Lebanon. He was also distressed by sectarian differences that tore the very fabric of society, tensions that he saw as often fueled by religious authorities. While passionately believing in the importance of cultivating peace, he felt strongly that "young nations like his own" should be freed from Ottoman control.

While some interpret his early writings as being against religion, they are not, per se, but rather against the hypocrisy, injustice, and self-aggrandizement done in the name of God. As Kahlil began to write with a righteous indignation, his reasons for not identifying with any church became clear. Kahlil instead chose to focus on "awakening" people to their greater selves and to the true heart of God.

As a result of his writing, Kahlil began to be seen by some as a "heretic and rebel," both religiously and politically. This is most clearly seen a few years later, when he moved to Paris for art studies, in the reaction to the Arabic publication of his book *Spirits Rebellious*. This collection of four stories, which includes a story titled "Khalil, the Heretic," resulted in significant controversy in the Arab world. *Spirits Rebellious* pulsates with righteous indignation and was immediately criticized by the Church for its antiestablishment tone and stance.

Although clerical disapproval of *Spirits Rebellious* was exaggerated after Kahlil's death to include accounts of his excommunication and book burnings, he did relate an unpleasant exchange between himself and a Maronite bishop to Mary Haskell, which she recorded in her journals.

> *Spirits Rebellious*, published while K. was in Paris, was suppressed by the Syrian government—only 200 copies got into Syria, secretly. Long since, of course, it has entered—and the edition has been exhausted. But the church considered excommunicating K. Practically he was excommunicated but the sentence was never actually pronounced. . . . When the representatives of the Patriarch, however, came to Paris they invited K. with other Syrians— and when he came to take leave asked him to stay and dine alone with them. One bishop had a sense of humor—the other none.
>
> Non-humorous took him aside: "You have made a grave mistake—are making a grave mistake. Your gifts you are using against your people, against your country, against your church. The holy Patriarch realizes this. But he does not condemn you. He sends

you a special message and loving offer of friendship. . . . And now—seek out every copy of the book—destroy them all—and let me take word from you back to Syria and the Church and to the holy Patriarch."[5]

This exchange only spurred Kahlil on further. The stories in *Spirits Rebellious* are bolder and his use of symbolism and imagery richer. All four short stories are set in rural Lebanon. Two deal with women forced into marriages by custom and tradition rather than out of love or spiritual affinity. Of these two, one ends with the woman leaving the wealth and security of her older husband to live in poverty with the man she loves; the other ends tragically, a la *Romeo and Juliet*. Another, "City of the Graves," dramatically confronts the condemning of innocents, corruption, and the oppression of the weak by the strong.

The pinnacle story, and one of my favorites, is "Khalil, the Heretic." It is a powerful, sweeping story with beautiful imagery, full of deep spiritual insight, delivering a triumphal tale in which greed, hypocrisy, and corruption are laid waste by the goodness and tender compassion of an oppressed people. All the elements of an epic drama are present, love story included, and the masterful expressions of a poet's heart pour forth in its descriptions of nature.

First we meet a "grand prince," Sheikh Abbas, squeezing life out of his vassal servants:

> The submission of these unfortunates to the Sheik Abbas and their fear of his harshness did not come only from his strength and their weakness, but it came from their poverty and reliance upon him. The fields they tilled and the hovels in which they dwelt belonged to him; they were a heritage from his father and grandfather as the people's heritage from their forefathers was poverty and wretchedness.[6]

As the scene is set at the outset of the story, the supporting character of the natural world plays its special role once again:

> Winter came with its snows and storms, and the fields and valleys were empty save for the croaking ravens and the naked trees. . . .

December drew to a close. The old year sighed and breathed its last minutes into the grey skies; then came night, wherein the new year was a child crowned by destiny and placed on the throne of existence.[7]

Next, our peasant hero Khalil, an orphan, is introduced:

On that terrible night beneath wild skies a youth of twenty and two years made his way along the road that rose gradually from the monastery of Kizhaya [here he's going for the jugular— Kizhaya was the richest and most famous monastery in Lebanon] to the village of the Sheik Abbas. The cold had dried up his very bones, and hunger and fear had sucked away his strength. Snow covered his black cloak as though wishing to make for him a shroud. . . .The rugged path seized hold of his feet and he fell. He called out for help, then was silenced by the cold.[8]

But all is not lost.

On that wild night already described, Rahel and her daughter were sitting by a fire whose heat was lost in the cold and whose embers were grey. Above their heads hung a lamp, which sent forth its feeble yellow rays into the gloom like a prayer that sends forth consolation into the hearts of the bereaved.[9]

Rescue is at hand, and a moving tale unfolds as the widow and her daughter save Khalil's life and he in turn awakens the village to their "greater selves," a theme woven into much of Kahlil's future art and writings. Shocked to discover that the monks of the monastery had thrown the orphan Khalil out into a snowy night, the women's apprehension soon fades as they discover the reasons for his banishment, essentially the living of too Christlike a life.

I left the monastery because I was not a blind and dumb being, but a man hearing and seeing. . . . The monks taught me to have no belief except in their way of life. They poisoned my soul with submission and despair until I reckoned the world an ocean of sorrow and misfortune and the monastery a port of salvation.[10]

True light is that which radiates from within a man. It reveals the secrets of the soul to the soul and lets it rejoice in life, singing in the name of the Spirit. Truth is like the stars, which cannot be seen except beyond the darkness of night. Truth is like all beautiful things in existence: it does not reveal its beauties save to those who have felt the weight of falsehood. Truth is a hidden feeling which teaches us to rejoice in our days and wish to all mankind that rejoicing.[11]

We come not to this world as outcasts, but as ignorant children, that we may learn from life's beauties and secrets the worship of the everlasting and universal spirit and the search after the hidden things of the soul. This is the truth as I knew it when I read the teachings of Jesus the Nazarene, and this is the light that emanated from within me and showed me the monastery and all in it as a black pit from whose depths rose frightening phantoms and images to destroy me.[12]

After an initial month's punishment of solitary confinement in the monastery's dungeon, Khalil soon realizes that the monks have not softened.

But vain was my thinking, for the thick veil that the long ages had woven across their eyes was not to be torn apart by a few days. And the clay with which ignorance had stopped their ears could not be moved by the soft touch of fingers.[13]

It is not surprising that such writing threatened the church hierarchy of Lebanon. Combined with the other stories in *Spirits Rebellious*, which also attacked traditional cultural mores, it is no wonder Kahlil was labeled a heretic.

Later in "Khalil, the Heretic," Khalil speaks to an audience of villagers while on trial before the unrelenting Sheik Abbas:

My crime, O men, is in my knowledge of your despair and my feeling for the weight of your fetters. And my sin, O women, is in my compassion for you and your children, who suck in life from your breasts with the sting of death. I am your kin, for my forefathers lived in these valleys that exhaust your strength and died under this yoke which bends your necks. I believe in God, who hears the cry of your tormented spirits and sees into your broken hearts. I believe in the Book that makes us all brothers equal before the sun. I believe in the teachings that free you and me from bondage and place us unfettered upon the earth, the stepping-place of the feet of God.[14]

God has surely sent your souls into this life to be as a lighted torch growing in knowledge and increasing in beauty in their search after the secrets of the days and the nights. . . . God has given to your spirits wings to soar aloft into the realms of love and freedom.[15]

His developing view of religious authorities, beyond just church leaders, is clearly seen in his longest work, a novella titled *Broken Wings*. He takes a pause in the story to verbally blast more than just the bishop:

The heads of religion in the East are not satisfied with their own munificence, but they must strive to make all members of their families superiors and oppressors. The glory of a prince goes to his eldest son by inheritance, but the exaltation of a religious head is contagious among his brothers and nephews. Thus the Christian bishop and the Moslem imam and the Brahmin priest become like sea reptiles who clutch their prey with many tentacles and suck their blood with numerous mouths.[16]

Not only do religious leaders receive a lashing, but the rulers of their lands are attacked as well:

Because of their wickedness and guile family was set against family; community against community; tribe against tribe. For how long shall we be scattered like dust before this cruel storm and quarrel like hungry whelps around this stinking corpse? The better to keep their thrones and ease of mind did they arm the Druse against the Arab and stir up the Shiite against the Sunnite and encourage the Kurd to slaughter the Bedouin and put Moslem to dispute with Christian. Until when will brother continue to slay brother on his mother's bosom? Until when will neighbor threaten neighbor by the grave of the beloved? Until when will the Cross be separated from the Crescent before the face of God?[17]

However, unlike his story "Yuhanna the Mad," this story ends in a hopeful tone.

Half a century has now passed since these happenings, and an awakening has come to the people of Lebanon.[18]

In 1908, addressing the Arab religious backlash against him, Kahlil wrote to a cousin living in Brazil:

I feel that the fires that feed the affection within me would like to dress themselves with ink and paper, but I am not sure whether the Arabic-speaking world would remain as friendly to me as it has been in the past three years. I say this because the apparition of enmity has already appeared. The people in Syria are calling me heretic, and the intelligentsia in Egypt vilified me, saying, "he is the enemy of just laws, of family ties, and of old traditions." Those writers are telling the truth, because I do not love man-made laws and I abhor the traditions that our ancestors left us. This hatred is the fruit of my love for the sacred and spiritual kindness which should be the source of every law upon the earth, for kindness is the shadow of God in man. I know that the principles upon which I base my writings are echoes of the spirit of the great majority of the people of the world, because the tendency towards a spiritual independence is to our life as the heart is to the body. . . . Will my teaching ever be received by the Arab world or will it die away and disappear like a shadow?[19]

A century has passed and Kahlil's words have not disappeared. Although considered a heretic and a rebel by some at the outset of his writing career, over time Kahlil's voice began to soften. After exposing the duplicity he observed in religion, he began to journey toward a deeper spirituality. He found harmony within and sought creative ways to share his discoveries with others. While seen early on as a heretic for his critique of the religious establishment, ironically his inclusive spirituality would be embraced by the world.

⸎

"Who is that man?" I heard a young girl ask her mother as she rubbed her little hand across the bronze bas-relief of Kahlil Gibran's youthful face on the public monument on Boston's historic Copley Square. "I don't know, but he must be famous," her mother responded. I interjected and asked her if she had heard of the book *The Prophet*. "Oh, yes," she replied. "That is one of my favorite books." "Well, he is the author," I pointed out. The woman leaned over and read the plaque, musing slowly over its words. She then took a photograph, carefully positioning her little girl in front of it. "Thank you," she said to me as she walked away, casually glancing back at the monument several times. Ironically, in the background of her photograph would be a church, the famous Trinity Episcopal Church, whose distinguished rector, Phillips Brooks, wrote the beloved Christmas Carol "O Little Town of Bethlehem." He died just a few years before Kahlil immigrated to Boston.

Standing in front of the memorial plaque aptly placed between Trinity Church and Boston's Public Library, which Kahlil frequented, I found myself contemplating the combination of influences on his life during his years in Boston. On the side of the granite memorial are engraved these words written by Kahlil: "It was in my heart to help a little because I was helped much." This young immigrant boy had come a long way.

The words engraved in the granite next to the bronze plaque say it all: "A grateful city acknowledges the greater harmony among men and strengthened universality of spirit given by Kahlil Gibran to the people of the world in return." This "citizen of Boston" would go on to inspire all to be "citizens of God's world."

The Lover   3

All these things shall love do unto you
That you may know the secrets of your heart,
And in that knowledge become a fragment of Life's heart.

—KAHLIL GIBRAN, *THE PROPHET*[1]

H E TAUGHT ME HOW TO SEE," I explained to Britelle, my daughter, as we looked out over the elegant expanse of the Jardin des Tuileries toward the Louvre. With our backs to the giant Egyptian hieroglyphed obelisk in the Place de la Concorde, the *jardin* was alive with springtime. It was early May. This was a view that Kahlil undoubtedly saw numerous times during the two and a half years he spent in Paris—every Sunday, when admission was free, Kahlil and his high school friend, Yusuf Huwayyik, would visit the Louvre. Kahlil described themselves "as pilgrims visiting a holy shrine."[2]

Growing up in French-speaking Senegal, formerly one of France's West African colonies, I was surrounded by many people who considered Paris the ultimate dream place to live. Our family often flew through France when we returned to visit the United States. Paris seemed to be a part of my world from my first remembrances. It was a place I knew quite intimately. However, it was not until I moved to Paris the summer after graduating from university that I was taught "how to see" its beauty. The city came to life for me when my flatmate, an artist, took the time to teach me to "see"—to observe the depth of colors, the distinctive shape of things; to detect the way light falls at different times of the day; to focus on that which others commonly do not notice. No city in the world could have been a better classroom for learning how to see than the City of Lights.

While there together, my daughter and I discovered Kahlil's Paris. We visited the homes of the writers Kahlil saw as role models, Honoré de Balzac and Victor Hugo. We explored the Left Bank's winding streets, strolled down the Boulevard du Montparnasse, had a café crème at the Dome Café in the Latin Quarter, discovered where Kahlil's last studio was on the Rue du Cherche-Midi, and walked the banks of the Seine at night—all important to his time in Paris. Standing in front of Kahlil's studio apartment at 14 Avenue du Maine, we read the plaque in French commemorating his time there: "Here lived from 1908 to 1910, Gibran Kahlil Gibran, 1883–1931, Painter and Poet, Lebanese-American."

Later in the day, as we dined at La Closerie des Lilas, where Kahlil used to sit with his fellow artist friends, we talked about that important learning time in my own life. My daughter quite wisely observed that learning how to see can be another way of learning how to love, for seeing things for their innate beauty and depth, whether people, places, things, or experiences, results in loving them most fully. Perhaps this is what Vincent van Gogh meant in a letter to his brother Theo in Paris in 1880, when he wrote, "I always think that the best way to know God is to *love many things*. Love a friend, a wife, something—whatever you like—you will be on the way to knowing more about Him. . . . But one must love with a lofty and serious sympathy with strength, with intelligence."[3] A year later Vincent put it this way: "To believe in God is to feel that there is a God . . . [who is] urging us towards *aimer encore* [loving more] with irresistible force."[4]

Moving to Paris in 1908, Kahlil fell in love with the city. His time in what is often referred to as the City of Love was an immensely formative period, profoundly influencing him for the rest of his life. It was a time when art thrived in Paris. Many of the great Impressionist artists were still there, albeit aging: Edgar Degas, Pierre-Auguste Renoir, Claude Monet, Mary Cassatt. It was also a period when "revolutionary elements" were influencing visual art. Georges Braque and Pablo Picasso, cofounders of Cubism, were in France at the time. The Fauvist movement of Henri Matisse and Georges Rouault was well under way. Even the young Russian modernist artist Marc Chagall moved to Paris while Kahlil was there. Some historians call this period in Paris "The Luminous Years."

There could not have been a more interesting time to be in this art capital of the world, and Kahlil matured greatly in both his art and thinking. Although artistically gifted, prior to Paris Kahlil lacked formal training. Painting was initially his primary expression of creativity, and while this came instinctively to him, his patron, Mary Haskell, realized the benefit that formal training could provide during this early stage of his artistic development. Her willingness to sponsor several years in Paris enabled Kahlil to explore the fundamentals of painting and introduced him to the concept of visionary art, educating him in the artistic genre of Symbolism. Symbolist art, a late-nineteenth-century artistic movement in which artists portrayed their own vision of existence, thereby becoming seers or prophets of sorts, had deeply personal and mystical components and often employed mythological and dream imagery.

Underscoring how important the subject of art was to Kahlil, he wrote:

> We have forgotten—or have we?—that there is but one universal language and that its voice is art.[5]

Kahlil wrote to Mary from Paris in October 1908:

> I am painting, or I am learning how to paint. It will take me a long time to paint as I want to, but it is beautiful to feel the growth of one's own vision of things. There are times when I leave work with the feelings of a child who is put to bed early.

> Do you not remember . . . my telling you that I understand
> people and things through my sense of hearing and that sound
> comes first to my soul? Now . . . I am beginning to understand
> things and people through my eyes.[6]

Not long into his formal art studies at L'Académie Julian, Kahlil
began to feel confined and frustrated by the rules and constraints
of a traditional art program. In another letter to Mary he describes
his angst:

> The professors in the academy are always saying to me "do not
> make the model more beautiful than she is." And my soul is al-
> ways whispering "O if you could only paint the model as beauti-
> ful as she really is."[7]

Some months later he was introduced to a new teacher, Pierre
Marcel-Beronneau, a visionary painter and disciple of the great
nineteenth-century artist Gustave Moreau, who is seen as a father of the Symbolist movement. Kahlil found in him a kindred
spirit—a mystic—and was encouraged to pour himself into the
rudiments of technical painting, yet with the freedom and ultimate
goal being self-expression. He also discovered the work of the
French Symbolist painter Eugène Carrière, who had died three
years earlier. Carrière's work was ethereal and deeply inspiring to
Kahlil. In another letter to Mary he wrote:

> The work of Carrière is nearest to my heart. His figures, sitting or
> standing behind the mist, say more to me than anything else except
> the work of Leonardo da Vinci. Carrière understood faces and
> hands more than any other painter. He knew the depths, the height,
> and the width of the human figure. And Carrière's life is not less
> beautiful than his work. He suffered much, but he understood the
> mystery of pain: he knew that tears make all things shine.[8]

It was during this time that Kahlil had the privilege of meeting
the great French sculptor Auguste Rodin, a close friend of the
late Carrière. Kahlil saw Rodin do with sculpture what Carrière
attempted to do on canvas. He was deeply inspired by the "spiri-

tuality" of Rodin's work. Kahlil's friend Mischa wrote of Kahlil's impression of Rodin: "He always marveled at the grand sweep of [Rodin's] imagination and the passing ease with which his chisel and his brush made bronze and stone and canvas burst with power, poetry, and the will of life to freedom."[9]

Nowhere is the transcendent nature of Rodin's work captured more beautifully than in Austrian poet Rainer Maria Rilke's long essay on the great sculptor. It is something I have personally gone back to time and time again. Rilke, in Paris at the same time as Kahlil, spent many hours with Rodin and worked as his personal secretary for a year. A mystic himself, Rilke highlighted in his work one of Rodin's most moving marble sculptures about love, titled *L'Éternelle Idole*. Focusing on the spiritual depth of the sculpture, Rilke wrote, "The material texture of this creation encloses a living impulse as a wall encloses a garden."[10] Interestingly, the painter whom Kahlil most idolized, Carrière, owned one of the copies of this moving sculpture and had it prominently displayed in his Parisian home. Attempting to describe it as it was positioned in the twilight, Rilke wrote:

> [T]his stone pulsates like a spring in which there is an eternal motion, a rising and falling, a mysterious stir of an elemental force . . . [it] radiates a mysterious greatness. One does not dare to give it one meaning, it has thousands. Thoughts glide over it like shadows, new meanings arise like riddles and unfold into clear significance. . . . A heaven is near that has not yet been reached, a hell is near that has not yet been forgotten. Here, too, all splendor flashes.[11]

I have visited the Musée Rodin several times. Its beautiful estate, with splendidly manicured gardens, is just a few blocks from where I first resided when living in Paris just after university. Today it contains the largest collection of the sculptor's works. After each visit I have come away deeply inspired. Walking in the gardens I am always struck by Rodin's moving sculpture *Fugit Amor* (Fugitive Love). The atmosphere is so inspiring that it makes many visitors believe even they can perhaps learn to sculpt.

During Kahlil's Parisian sojourn, what is today the Musée Rodin was then the Hôtel Biron. It was a somewhat dilapidated building that, while up for sale, allowed tenants. Among them were several prominent writers and artists, including the painter Henri Matisse. One of the artists was a young sculptress named Clara Westhoff, Rilke's future wife. Clara told Rodin about the estate, and in 1908, the year Kahlil moved to Paris, Rodin began renting four south-facing ground-floor rooms opening onto the terrace to use as his studios. The gorgeous garden that one sees today was at that time allowed to run wild, and Rodin saw it as a space to place some of his works. Gradually Rodin took over more of the building, and by 1911 he was the sole occupant, residing there for the rest of his life.

It is here that Kahlil once spent an hour in Rodin's studio, together with professors and students. During a question-and-answer period, the great sculptor spoke of William Blake, the early-eighteenth-century English poet and artist who is considered one of the most original Romantic visual artists. Rodin spoke of Blake's life and how the muses of art and poetry combined to give him a complete artistic expression, enhancing his art with poetry and his poetry with art. Rodin was echoing the saying of the ancient Roman Horace: *ut pictura poesis* ("as is painting so is poetry"). Kahlil left Rodin's studio and went straight to an English bookshop, found a copy of Blake's works, and spent the rest of the day at the Jardin du Luxembourg on the Left Bank obsessively devouring Blake's art and poetry; he had discovered a companion for his spiritual and artistic journey.

During his time in Paris, Kahlil journeyed to London and while there absorbed himself in Blake's paintings and etchings at the Tate Gallery. Years later, when Kahlil's publications were being marketed by Alfred A. Knopf, an up-and-coming American publisher, it was said that Rodin himself referred to Kahlil as the "William Blake of the twentieth century," a claim that cannot be verified. Yet one significant artistic project that Kahlil initiated in Paris was his *Temple of Art* series of pencil portraits of famous artists of the day. Central to this series was a commanding portrait of Rodin, which I saw in Bsharri.

In 1910, during his last spring in Paris, one of Kahlil's oil paintings, his medium of art in Paris, was entered in a show of the Société Nationale des Beaux-Arts. Entitled *Autumn*, it is said to be of Micheline, a French romantic interest he had first met in Boston who had helped him get settled in Paris. Like many of his works, the subject's eyes are closed, as if in an appeal to look deeper than the surface of beauty into the soul. Rather than a defining portrait, it is an inspiring work full of movement and feeling, authentic and in harmony with his style of expression. While Kahlil was unhappy with his painting's location in the exhibition hall, he was thrilled to see Rodin visiting the exhibition. Rodin recognized him, and they spoke briefly; the sculptor even stopped for a moment in front of his painting. Kahlil truly held Rodin in awe. It is fitting that today the largest collections of both Rodin's and Kahlil's works in the Western Hemisphere are exhibited next to each other at the fabulous Soumaya Museum in Mexico City.

Of Kahlil's art, his friend Mischa wrote:

> [A]s an artist he always sought simplicity of form and execution which gave his works that intriguing lightness and transparency. It was a classical simplicity which had a firm grasp of the basic fundamentals of art without being conscious of the fact; a simplicity that with a few lines would create many shapes. Far from being boundaries to the looker's imagination those lines were eyes and wings that carried the looker leagues and leagues beyond themselves.[12]

While in Paris, albeit distanced from Mary, his admiration and love for her continued to grow. As their frequent letters attest, the sharing of their inner lives was deepening. Upon his return to Boston after the two-year separation, he proposed marriage to her. At first she refused, the societal complexities too great, and then she changed her mind. After much angst for them both, they ultimately settled into a platonic relationship sustained by the companionship of their souls. They resonated deeply on a spiritual level, and Mary remained his benefactor all his life and finally the guardian of his work after death.

Throughout this period his contact with the Arabic literary world was flourishing. For several years he had contributed work to the New York newspaper *al-Mohajer* (The Emigrant), which was reaching audiences across the Arab world. While in Paris he worked on a semi-autobiographical novella titled *Broken Wings*, which was eventually published in 1912. More than any of his other writings, the pages of *Broken Wings* strongly express Kahlil's love for life, for women, and for God. It was a work that also led to "meeting" another profound love in his life, May Ziadah, who had moved to Cairo the year Kahlil moved to Paris. She was a gifted young writer, born in Nazareth in 1886. Her father was a Lebanese teacher from a village in the north of Lebanon; her mother was Palestinian. She grew up in Lebanon, but in 1908 her family moved to Egypt, where her father became the editor of a newspaper. Unusually talented with a command of English, French, and Arabic, she made a name for herself in journalism and literature. She was a committed feminist and hosted a weekly literary salon of contemporary Arab intellectuals in her home, attended by some of the Arab world's greatest writers. These included Taha Hussein, known as "The Dean of Arabic Literature" and one of the most influential twentieth-century Egyptian writers and intellectuals, and Ahmed Lutfi el-Sayed, termed "Professor of the Generation." He was the first director of Cairo University and an architect of modern Egyptian nationalism.

After reading Kahlil's novella *Broken Wings*, May wrote to him expressing admiration for his writings, to which Kahlil responded, beginning an intense and lifelong correspondence. Like Kahlil, May never married, and although they never met in person, they exchanged letters regularly and a love grew between them that continued until his death nineteen years later. While Kahlil's letters to her over the years have been compiled into a book, her family never gave permission for hers to be published. Most importantly, May is credited with introducing Kahlil's work to the Egyptian public.

Kahlil Gibran is still a household name in today's Cairo, a vast city of more than twenty million people, where I lived for ten years. Along the banks of the ancient Nile, Cairo is often referred to as the "capital of the Middle East" due to its cultural, political, and religious influence. Egypt is the center of the Arab world's film and publishing industry and is also the home of Al-Azhar, the intellectual and spiritual heart of Sunni Islam, counting more than 90 percent of all Muslims in the world. It also has the largest and oldest indigenous Christian community in the Middle East, the ancient Coptic Orthodox Church, numbering up to ten million people. I was there as the rector of the English-speaking international church, St. John's Episcopal Church, which had been founded in 1931 and over the years had become a creative catalyst for building bridges between the cultures and creeds of the Middle East and the West. As the arts can be one of the most effective mediums to build bridges between the faiths of the East and West, we held numerous interfaith programs focusing on visual art, film, literature, and music.

Literary salons continue to play an influential role in Egyptian public discourse. Throughout the history of the Middle East, salons have provided forums where citizens conspired, formed alliances, and critiqued their country's leaders. The most celebrated literary gatherings in the Arab world, which I once had the privilege of attending in Cairo, were hosted by the late Egyptian novelist and Nobel laureate Naguib Mahfouz. Today, however, the most prominent literary salons are hosted by the renowned Egyptian novelist and writer Dr. Alaa Al Aswany, whose novel *The Yacoubian Building* captured the world's attention. An outspoken political and social commentator and one of Egypt's best-known public intellectuals, Al Aswany's writings played a crucial role in triggering the revolutionary sentiments among the Egyptian people in early 2011. Al Aswany was one of the few prominent faces of the leaderless demonstrations in the now-famous Tahrir Square, which lasted eighteen days and ended on February 11, when President Hosni Mubarak was toppled.

During my years in Cairo, the distressing days of the 2011 Egyptian Revolution were by far the most memorable. With all telephone and Internet communications with the outside world purposely cut off by the regime during the early days of the protests, there was a sense of deep uncertainty as to what was really happening. We experienced a few traumatic nights, as did millions of residents of Egypt's largest cities, as thugs attempted numerous times to enter our apartment building, only to be warded off by our Egyptian neighbors' shotguns. CNN's global news coverage actually highlighted the various attempts by bandit mobs carrying knives, two-by-fours, and makeshift weapons to breach our building. Soon neighborhood vigilante groups formed throughout the cities to protect their respective neighborhoods, as all police and government security had disappeared. These were harrowing days in many ways.

Just under a month after President Mubarak's ouster, I found myself in downtown Cairo, standing in a crowded smoke-filled room for Al Aswany's first post-Mubarak salon. He had been holding this weekly literary salon for more than fifteen years, but this one was different. More than one hundred political activists, artists, academics, businesspersons, and youths packed the room to hear his perspective on the current political situation. Most of the discussions revolved around the seemingly real possibility of building democracy in Egypt.

Banners surrounded the entrance to the meeting room, carrying everything from popular revolutionary slogans to publicity for Coca-Cola. But the central banner, visible to everyone, held the words of Kahlil Gibran in Arabic, about what good "citizenship" entails:

> It is to acknowledge the other person's rights before asserting your own; but always to be conscious of your own. It is to be free in word, and deed; but it is also to know that your freedom

is subject to the other person's freedom. It is to create the useful and the beautiful with your own hands and to admire what others have created in love and with faith. It is to produce by labour and only by labour and to spend less than you have produced that your children may not be dependent upon the state for support when you are no more.[13]

May would have been extremely proud.

Broken Wings, the longest narrative Kahlil ever wrote, is a tender lyrical story of love that flies in the face of the Middle Eastern cultural traditions of his time. Exploring the contrasting colors of joy and sorrow, he used brushstrokes of compassion to insightfully portray both love's happiness as well as immeasurable sorrow in a search for spiritual meaning.

It was actually Kahlil's defense of the rights of "her oppressed sisters in the East" that most impressed May in *Broken Wings*. Kahlil embraced an incredibly high view of women, whether friend, stranger, lover, sister, or mother, and he consistently wove his admiration for them into the essence of his painting and writing. This is especially noteworthy considering the patriarchal society of his childhood, and also the time period in America in which he was immersed, as women were in the thick of the fight for the right to vote. Even his view of God echoed his convictions and pushed the boundaries of the accepted norm:

> Most religions speak of God in the masculine gender. To me He is as much a Mother as He is a Father. He is both the father and the mother in one; and Woman is the God-Mother. The God-Father may be reached through the mind or the imagination. But the God-Mother can be reached through the heart only—through love.[14]

He also wrote affectionately of mothers and drew the image of his own mother in a moving work of art called *Towards the Infinite*, the frontispiece of a published collection of his art titled *Twenty Drawings*. In *Broken Wings* he lifted the role of "mother" onto the highest pedestal.

> The most beautiful word on the lips of mankind is the word "Mother," and the most beautiful call is the call of "My mother." It is a word full of hope and love, a sweet and kind word coming from the depths of the heart. The mother is everything—she is our consolation in sorrow, our hope in misery, and our strength in weakness. She is the source of love, mercy, sympathy, and forgiveness. He who loses his mother loses a pure soul who blesses and guards him constantly.[15]
>
> Every thing in nature bespeaks the mother. The sun is the mother of earth and gives it its nourishment of heat; it never leaves the universe at night until it has put the earth to sleep to the song of the sea and the hymn of birds and brooks. And this earth is the mother of trees and flowers. It produces them, nurses them, and weans them. The trees and flowers become kind mothers of their great fruits and seeds. And the mother, the prototype of all existence, is the eternal spirit, full of beauty and love.[16]

Kahlil, reflecting on his mother, wrote, "She lived countless poems and never wrote one. . . . The song that lies silent in the heart of the mother will sing upon the lips of the child." And in the wake of her death, he said, "My life is shrouded, not because she was my mother, but because she was my friend."[17]

In the opening pages of *Broken Wings*, Kahlil invites us into the silent sorrow of an older man as he recalls the loss of his great love in his youth. The hand of destiny led the man early in life to his heart's "shrine," Selma.

> In that year I was reborn and unless a person is born again his life will remain like a blank sheet in the book of existence. In that year, I saw the angels of heaven looking at me through the eyes of a beautiful woman.[18]
>
> Real beauty is a ray which emanates from the holy of holies of the spirit, and illuminates the body, as life comes from the depths of the earth and gives color and scent to a flower.[19]

The sorrowful spirit finds rest when united with a similar one. . . . Hearts that are united through the medium of sorrow will not be separated by the glory of happiness. Love that is cleansed by tears will remain eternally pure and beautiful.[20]

Just as love is blossoming, Selma's widowed father is visited by an imposing bishop, shattering the old man's world with his request for the hand of his daughter for a nephew in need of a wife. The father's only response to the bishop was a deep silence and falling tears.

The father emerges from this meeting bent down, as if carrying a heavy load, and in tears tries to tell his daughter she is going to be taken away.

> Hearing these words, Selma's face clouded and her eyes froze as if she felt a premonition of death. Then she screamed, like a bird shot down, suffering, and trembling, and in a choked voice said, "What do you say? What do you mean? Where are you sending me?"
>
> Then she looked at him searchingly, trying to discover his secret. In a moment she said, "I understand. I understand everything. The Bishop has demanded me from you and has prepared a cage for this bird with broken wings."[21]

After a week passes, the young man searches for perspective as he processes what is to come. We get a subtle glimpse here of Kahlil's intentional insertion of joy in the midst of sorrow, a sort of swaying back and forth in the rhythmic dance of life.

> In the morning, when I walked in the fields, I saw the token of Eternity in the awakening of nature, and when I sat by the seashore I heard the waves singing the song of Eternity. And when I walked in the streets I saw the beauty of life and the splendor of humanity in the appearance of passers-by and the movements of workers.[22]

Before the two lovers are forced to part ways, each speaks in turn:

> Then she said, "I want you to love me as a poet loves his sorrowful thoughts. I want you to remember me as a traveller remembers a calm pool in which his image was reflected as he

drank its water. I want you to remember me as a mother remembers her child that died before it saw the light, and I want
you to remember me as a merciful king remembers a prisoner
who died before his pardon reached him. I want you to be my
companion, and I want you to visit my father and console him
in his solitude because I shall be leaving him soon and shall be
a stranger to him."[23]

I answered her, saying, "I will do all you have said and will
make my soul an envelope for your soul, and my heart a residence for your beauty and my breast a grave for your sorrows. I
shall love you, Selma, as the prairies love the spring, and I shall
live in you in the life of a flower under the sun's rays. I shall
sing your name as the valley sings the echo of the bells of the
village churches; I shall listen to the language of your soul as the
shore listens to the story of the waves. I shall remember you as a
stranger remembers his beloved country, and as a hungry man remembers a banquet, and as a dethroned king remembers the days
of his glory, and as a prisoner remembers the hours of ease and
freedom. I shall remember you as a sower remembers the bundles
of wheat on his threshing floor, and as a shepherd remembers the
green prairies, the sweet brooks."[24]

Later in *Broken Wings*, on his deathbed Selma's father declares:

> Let my dream end and my soul awaken with the dawn.[25]
> Oh, Lord, have mercy and mend our broken wings.[26]

For some time after Selma's marriage, the two lovers arranged to
meet, chastely, in the ruins of an old temple, until suspicions arose.
The setting is symbolic; on one wall is painted a crucified Christ
with his mother and women sorrowfully at his side, and on the
other is an old Phoenician picture carved into the rock depicting
Ishtar, goddess of love and beauty, sitting on her throne.

During one visit Selma points out:

> In the heart of this rock there are two symbols depicting the
> essence of a woman's desires and revealing the hidden secrets of
> her soul, moving between love and sorrow—between affection
> and sacrifice, between Ishtar sitting on the throne and Mary

standing by the cross. The man buys glory and reputation, but the woman pays the price.[27]

Human society has yielded for seventy centuries to corrupted laws until it cannot understand the meaning of the superior and eternal laws. A man's eyes have become accustomed to the dim light of candles and cannot see the sunlight. Spiritual disease is inherited from one generation to another until it has become a part of people, who look upon it, not as a disease, but as a natural gift, showered by God upon Adam. If those people found someone free from the germs of this disease, they would think of him with shame and disgrace.[28]

This tender tale finds an appropriately tragic ending with the death of Selma and her newborn. Yet infused throughout are the vacillating emotions and expressions of joy and sorrow. To Kahlil this theme permeated so much of his worldview and, in turn, his art and writing. In the face of personal suffering, he allowed himself to feel deeply; but in that same well of depth, he found its counterpart—the beauty of joy. He was a lover of life, not primarily in the surface layer of happiness abounding, although he undoubtedly experienced such moments, but in a fuller, richer sense.

"'Seeing through the Eye,' old boy, is the secret," a wise old sage told me as he put his hand on my shoulder; his sparkling blue eyes seemed to penetrate my soul. Working in London not long after university, I had taken the Saturday train down to the village of Robertsbridge in East Sussex to meet one of my heroes, Malcolm Muggeridge, the English writer, mystic, and former BBC commentator. He was eighty-five years of age, with only several years left to live. Yet there in his quaint country cottage, he pointedly wanted to share the lessons he had learned over the course of his fascinating and at times troubled life. "Seeing through the Eye."

It was a line from a poem by the nineteenth-century English poet and artist William Blake, whom Muggeridge, like Kahlil, was very keen on and had written about extensively. Muggeridge introduced me to William Blake that day, as Rodin introduced Kahlil to him in Paris. Interestingly, Muggeridge was pointing me to what is very much the theme of Kahlil's *Broken Wings*. As one reads *Broken Wings*, one senses the influence of Blake throughout. Blake had himself experienced profound states of celebration and desperation throughout his life. Muggeridge, like Blake, as the young Kahlil was learning, understood that Joy and Suffering are the two poles between which the current of life passes. Yet they can also together generate a spark of the Divine.

Muggeridge's favorite lines of Blake's poetry, lines I have become very fond of as well, certainly would have also captured Kahlil's attention.

> Man was made for Joy & Woe,
> And when this we rightly know,
> Thro' the World we safely go.
> Joy & Woe are woven fine,
> Clothing for the Soul divine;
> Under every grief & pine
> Runs a joy with silken twine.
> Every Night & every Morn
> Some to Misery are Born.
>
> Every Morn & every Night
> Some are born to sweet delight.
> Some are born to sweet delight,
> Some are born to Endless Night.
> We are led to Believe a Lie
> When we see not Thro' the Eye.[29]
>   ("Auguries of Innocence," 1803)

Kahlil very poignantly captures in *Broken Wings* this same paradox of life, in which deep joy is intertwined with profound sorrow.

As I left that day, heading back to the train station, I was reminded of a speech Muggeridge had given at my alma mater a number of years earlier. In it he concluded, "I can say with complete truthfulness that everything I have learned . . . in the world, everything that has truly enhanced and enlightened my existence, has been through affliction and not through happiness."

The life gift of joy and sorrow is a theme that Kahlil addresses in his writings throughout the rest of his life. In his work "The Spirit," from his collection *A Tear and a Smile*, Kahlil creatively explores this mystery more fully.

> And the God of gods separated a spirit from Himself and
>   created in it Beauty.
> He gave to it the lightness of the breeze at dawn and the
>   fragrance of the flowers of the field and the softness of
>   moonlight.
> Then He gave to it a cup of joy, saying:
> "You shall not drink of it except that you forget the Past
>   and heed not the Future."
> And He gave to it a cup of sadness, saying:
> "You shall drink and know therefrom the meaning of
>   Life's rejoicing."[30]
> Love, which is God, will accept from us these tears and
>   sighs as an offering . . .
>   (*A Tear and a Smile*)[31]

In other writings, Kahlil elaborates on this life mystery.

> For he who has not looked on Sorrow will never see Joy.
>   (*The Voice of the Master*)[32]

> When either your joy or your sorrow becomes great the
> world becomes small.
>   (*Sand and Foam*)[33]

> Sorrow softens the feelings, and Joy heals the wounded
> heart. Were Sorrow and Poverty abolished, the spirit of
> man would be like an empty tablet, with naught inscribed
> save the signs of selfishness and greed.
>> (*The Voice of the Master*)[34]

> Your joy is sorrow unmasked.
>> (*The Prophet*)[35]

> He was a man of joy; and it was upon the path of joy that
> He met the sorrows of all men. And it was from the high
> roofs of His sorrows that He beheld the joy of all men.
>> (*Jesus the Son of Man*)[36]

Kahlil resonated with Blake's spirituality as well as his art and writing. While Blake's work often attacked conventional religion, his rejection of religiosity was not a rejection of spirituality. And Blake, like Kahlil, admired Jesus profoundly, seeing him as above all dogma and morality.

Despite the fact that Kahlil did not resonate with the forms of a traditional religion and repeatedly blasted hypocrisy in religious institutions, such as utilizing the role of a bishop as the "bad guy" in *Broken Wings*, he was a deeply spiritual person with a profound love for God. From his earliest years on, he refused to limit his concept of God, rooted in him through the gift of his mother, but rather sought persistently to quench his longings for God.

He once expressed to Mary, "When I paint a picture, I try to give the picture a presence. It is the coming together of certain elements in a certain way, as if they made a sort of path along which God can come through to our consciousness."[37] Another time he wrote to her, "I have obtained a first-rate telescope, and I spend an hour or two every evening staring into infinity, close to that which is distant and remote, and in awe of the Greater Whole."[38]

The collection of imagery and created synonyms Kahlil used for God are many: The Infinite, The Almighty, God Creator, Nature, Love, Spirit, Holy Spirit, Eternal Wisdom, Unseen, Supreme Poet, Eternal Altar, All-Powerful, Eternal Spirit, Supreme Infinite, Lord of Life of Love and of Death, Great Spirit, Great Intelligent Being, the Unknown, the Great Sea, the Absolute, Great Power, to name a few.

Over and over again Kahlil focused in his work on love for God rather than religion:

> "Religion?" in answer to a query. "What is it? I know only life. Life means the field, the vineyard and the loom. . . . The Church is within you. You yourself are your priest."[39]

Kahlil's friend Barbara Young was often asked about Kahlil's perspective on God and religion. In her reflections on Kahlil she wrote:

> Organized religion had no attraction for this man. He would not argue the subject. When some ardent cultist would seek to convince him of the supervalue of a particular creed or dogma, the poet would answer, "Yes, it is all on the way."[40]
>
> The question has been constantly asked me, "But was not Gibran really a Christian?" My own reply would be that he was the greatest Christian of them all—but neither an organized nor an orthodox Christian. Perhaps if we must have a word—he did not need one—we might call him a Christian mystic. For mystic he certainly was in the perfect and perfected sense.[41]

Kahlil was also a lover of great interior depth.

> "The soul is mightier than space," he said, "stronger than time, deeper than the sea, and higher than the stars." He was preoccupied during his entire life with the depths that he knew the spirit of man able to plumb and the heights that he was convinced man was destined to scale.[42]

He lived from within, passionately and intensely, exploring the rich reservoir of inner resources he had been given. To discover these gifts and share them was his passion. His work was his life, and with intensity of spirit, it gave the breath of creation to each of his tasks. Once asked by an admirer if he preferred writing or painting more, he responded by saying that was like asking someone which of his two children was his favorite. His time of development in Paris matured him on many levels, giving him more tools of expression and a greater understanding of who he was, as well as the permission to listen to the spiritual and creative foundations that had been whispering within him since his earliest days. He wrote to a friend a couple of years later, reflecting on the time in Paris, saying, "In Paris I was reborn."[43] Kahlil returned to Boston from Paris with confidence and clarity of vision. He would spend the remainder of his life giving expression to the creative fire of love within him.

In a letter to Mary on his birthday a few years later, he wrote:

> I have been thinking of writing, of giving forms, to the one thought that changed my inner-life—God and the Earth and the soul of man. A voice is shaping itself in my soul and I am waiting for words. My one desire now is to find the right form, the right garment that would cling to the human ears. The world is hungry, Mary; and if this *thing* is bread it will find a place in the heart of the world, and if it is not bread, it will at least make the hunger of the world deeper and higher. It is beautiful to speak of God to man. We cannot fully understand the nature of God because we are *not* God, but we can make ready our consciousness to understand, and grow through, the visible expressions of God.[44]

Paris profoundly shaped Kahlil's view on the fuller dimensions of love. While in Paris he began writing what was to become, years later, his magnum opus, *The Prophet*, his best-known work. It is composed of prose poetry essays addressing numerous topics. And in it Kahlil focuses first on Love, expressing his matured understanding of its meaning and depth.

> And think not you can direct the course of love, for love,
>   if it finds you worthy, directs your course.
> Love has no other desire but to fulfill itself.
> But if you love and must needs have desires, let these be
>   your desires:

To melt and be like a running brook that sings its melody
  to the night.
To know the pain of too much tenderness.
To be wounded by your own understanding of love;
And to bleed willingly and joyfully.
To wake at dawn with a winged heart and give thanks for
  another day of loving;
To rest at the noon hour and meditate love's ecstasy;
To return home at eventide with gratitude;
And then to sleep with a prayer for the beloved in your
  heart and a song of praise upon your lips.[45]

The Madman

4

The human heart cries out for help;
the human soul implores us for deliverance;
but we do not heed their cries,
for we neither hear nor understand.
But the man who hears and understands we call mad,
and flee from him

—KAHLIL GIBRAN, *THE VOICE OF THE MASTER*[1]

ONE OF MY DEAREST DREAMS IS THIS—somewhere, a body of work, say fifty or seventy-five pictures will be hung together in a large city, where people would see and perhaps love them. Oh it feels so good and so warm when ever I think of that."[2]

Kahlil wrote these words to Mary Haskell early in 1913. Unbeknownst to him, Kahlil was on the threshold of his notoriety as an artist and writer when he returned from Paris. In New York City I decided to first visit the famous, now infamous and closed, Knoedler & Co. gallery on East 70th Street on the Upper East Side. Founded in 1846, it was one of the oldest galleries in the United States. During Kahlil's time it was located on Fifth Avenue, and there he held his second major exhibition in New York.

It was the most notorious gallery then to show his art. Centaurs, dancers, mothers, and children were his chosen motifs.

I had written the gallery director ahead of my visit, highlighting the fact that Kahlil had exhibited at their gallery in 1917, explaining I was writing a book on Kahlil and inquiring into the possibility of looking at their archives. I never heard back from the director and so decided to drop in unannounced.

The day of my visit, the gallery was in the midst of an exhibition of "The Red Paintings (1962–1963)" by the late Jewish-American artist Michael Goldberg, an abstract expressionist painter. A contemporary of Willem de Kooning, Jackson Pollock, Franz Kline, and Mark Rothko, Goldberg came into prominence in the 1950s. It was quite a spectacular solo exhibition, his ten canvases large and rich in texture. I recall the prices ranging from $80,000 to $225,000.

While there I asked to see the director but was told he was unavailable. The attendant didn't seem interested in the fact that their gallery had exhibited Kahlil's work. I found myself perplexed by the lack of attention. Unbeknownst to me at that time, the gallery had already become a center of controversy in the art world and would soon shutter its windows and permanently close its doors amid rumors of selling forged paintings. Three former clients of the gallery ended up suing it for more than forty million dollars, arguing that they were duped into buying forged paintings that were attributed to renowned artists Jackson Pollock, Mark Rothko, and Willem de Kooning.

Not long after his return from Paris to Boston, Kahlil began working on the manuscript for his first book in English, *The Madman*. After the grand scale of artistic stimulation in Paris, Kahlil soon found Boston stifling. Although not wanting to leave his sister

Marianna, in 1911 he started to visit New York for long periods of time.

Kahlil's spirituality continued to mature as he explored creative and moving ways to communicate through his writing. While pursuing his passion for painting, he continued to publish his work in Arabic, releasing a compilation of short stories and poems in 1914 titled *A Tear and a Smile*. "A Vision," one of his moving short parables from *A Tear and a Smile*, describes a bird that has died of thirst in its cage near the banks of a stream. In a very real sense, Kahlil is discovering his own wings, realizing what is holding him down and searching for a way to communicate life and freedom to others with the gifts he was given.

In a short story called "Before the Throne of Beauty," he wrote:

> You fear the God of all gods, and attribute to Him envy and malice.
> Yet what is He if not love and compassion?[3]

While Kahlil worked on *The Madman*, he began to demonstrate his natural gravitation to and admiration for eccentric individuals, artists, writers, and spiritual leaders, those often perceived as having alternative visions on life and spirituality—those "outside the norm" in the way they saw the world and communicated what they saw. In a letter to Mary, Kahlil wrote, "And what can I tell you of New York? . . . I have met many people [with] a saintly respect for art—people who are hungry for the beautiful and the *uncommon*."[4] During this time Kahlil met Irish poet and playwright and future Nobel laureate William Butler Yeats. Kahlil painted his portrait; Yeats's friend, Lady Gregory, was impressed with the portrait and sat for him as well. Their paths would cross several times over the coming years.

With continued financial support from Mary and introductions to friends in New York, Kahlil was eventually able to move into a building in Greenwich Village at 51 West 10th Street, said to be the first in America to be built exclusively for the use of painters and sculptors. The building is no longer there and has been replaced with a modern and quite drab-looking apartment building. As I stood outside the entrance looking up at the structure, a couple came out to walk their dog and asked if I needed assistance, as a number code is required to enter. I responded by asking them if they had ever heard of Kahlil Gibran. The woman lit up, saying, "Of course; I have *The Prophet* upstairs!" However, they had no idea he had lived there and seemed astounded to learn that where their building now stood was once a hub for many of New York's greatest artists.

It was a time of artistic stimulation and opportunity for Kahlil as his creative expressions developed. The arts and cultural life of the city inspired him. During the first part of the twentieth century, Greenwich Village itself was the heart of progressive, artistic, and political movements in the United States. In keeping with the theme of "the mad or reclusive monk," he called his studio apartment "The Hermitage," perhaps foreshadowing his increasingly solitary life as his best work began to emerge.

While he worked on *The Madman,* the world itself seemed to go mad. Weighing heavily on his mind were the tensions in Lebanon under the Ottoman occupation as the First World War loomed ahead. Kahlil began to see himself as somewhat of a "revolutionary" during this period. Through his writings he urged his people to remove the Ottoman yoke from their homeland. Later, during the war, he composed a public letter to Arab Muslims in which he implored Arabs, both Christian and Muslim, to combine forces against the oppressive Ottoman Turks.

One of Kahlil's neighbors was a portrait painter named Juliet Thompson. Her father had been a close friend of Abraham Lincoln, and she herself was a devoted follower of the Baha'i faith. She lent Kahlil some of the works of Baha'i founder Bahá'u'lláh. Resonating deeply with his message of unity and spiritual truths held in common across religions, he told Juliet it was "the most stupendous literature that ever was written."[5]

Having been to the beautiful Baha'i temples in New Delhi, India, Haifa, Israel, and Wilmette, Illinois, I can well understand what Kahlil felt. Each is seen as a house of worship for all peoples. The Baha'i faith believes in the unity of all people and faiths under God. Many around the world have been attracted to a faith that believes we all belong to one race, that all faiths share a common source and aim, and that God's long-awaited peace is within reach. While I was living in Egypt, one of my neighbors was of the Baha'i tradition. Sadly, the Baha'i were seen as a threat to governmental, Muslim, and Christian leadership. Despite the fact that they were monotheistic, the government denied the Baha'i legal registration status as a religion.

Juliet hosted 'Abdu'l-Bahá, the oldest son of the founder and the leader of the Baha'i at that time, when he visited the United States. She often referred to him as "the Master" and introduced Kahlil to him, asking him to do his portrait. Juliet loved Kahlil's artwork and described it with appreciation:

> His drawings were more beautiful than his paintings. These were very misty, lost things—mysterious and lost. Very poetic.[6]

The morning the *Titanic* sank on Tuesday, April 15, 1912, Kahlil, although deeply disturbed, kept his appointment to draw 'Abdu'l-Bahá. He later wrote to Mary:

> I went to sleep at 3:30 this morning. The air was so charged with the horrible sea tragedy that I was not able to go to sleep earlier. At 6:30 I was up. Cold water and strong coffee brought light to my eyes. At 7:30 I was with 'Abdu'l-Bahá.[7]

As 'Abdu'l-Bahá sat for Kahlil, they struck up a friendship. Kahlil later wrote of him to Mary:

> He is a very great man. He is complete. There are worlds in his soul. And oh what a remarkable face—what a beautiful face—so real and so sweet.[8]

Later Kahlil told Juliet that when he worked on his book *Jesus the Son of Man*, he thought of 'Abdu'l-Bahá throughout his time of writing.

In 1913 Kahlil met and drew Swiss psychiatrist Carl Jung, whom he came to admire, and was introduced to Jung's analytical psychology. About this time Mary introduced Kahlil to the poetic writings of that year's winner of the Nobel Prize for Literature, Rabindranath Tagore. She gave him Tagore's *Song Offerings*, a collection of devotional poems to the Supreme. Kahlil was much impressed with the deep-rooted spiritual essence of the work and its Eastern flavor. Tagore, whom Kahlil would also have the opportunity to meet some years later, was an imposing figure, with a long white beard and wild eyes, wearing robes, a sort of "ethereal Rasputin."[9]

I have visited Shantiniketan in Bengal, India, the ashram founded by Tagore in 1901. Under Tagore's leadership, it became India's first university township and eco-commune. Today the lush greenery and beautifully designed campus is witness to Tagore's vision for Shantiniketan to be a place of knowledge and universal spiritual brotherhood. Tagore profoundly believed that one's sensory encounter with the environment was as significant as the mind's inquiry into the world's inner mystery. He entrusted the task of creating an aesthetic setting, reflective of this vision, to the then-renowned artist Nandalal Bose. As I walked through the property, passing mud-brick buildings, tree-lined streets, and frescoes, I sensed a distinct spiritual aura to the place, enhanced all the more by its profound simplicity. It was hard not to imagine, in the mystical quietness of the place, the great poet-seer himself, that Tolstoyan figure, walking among the banyan trees.

When *The Madman* was first released, literary critics and reviewers often compared Kahlil to Tagore, as a sort of Middle Eastern counterpart. *The Madman* was a concerted effort with Mary's editorial assistance. It was again an example of how, together, they were able to touch sacred ground. The frontispiece of the book, titled *The Three Are One*, symbolized the actualization of their cooperative efforts.

As a child, growing up in the Qadisha Valley, Kahlil had visited one of the monasteries near his village where the "mad," those believed to be possessed, were housed. Alexandre Najjar, the Lebanese novelist and contemporary biographer of Kahlil, writes, "The most striking spot in this valley is undoubtedly the Monastery of Saint Anthony of Qoshaya, known for having one of the first printing presses in the East and where it was, until the last century, common practice to chain madmen to rocks in a deep, dark cave at the entrance of the monastery in the belief that their demons would be exorcised."[10]

During my own childhood in Senegal, I remember seeing *les fous* (madmen) roaming the streets. They were often dirty, with matted hair, and usually stark naked. They seemed strange and dangerous to me as a child. Ironically, in popular African folklore, they are often viewed as seers, reminiscent of that wild biblical seer John the Baptist, who we are told looked as wild as the wilderness itself. Rodin, in a deeply moving sculpture that Kahlil no doubt saw while in Paris, captures the roughness and rawness of John the Baptist—wild-eyed, lean like a desert cactus, in picturesque costume on the bank of the Jordan River.

The childhood images of these outcasts stayed with Kahlil, and he once told Mary of an incident in which he admired the wisdom of a madman.

> Once when I was riding with a companion we came upon a madman who was well known in all the country round as mad, but harmless. It was the time of year when all the people were busy, getting in the harvest. But he was standing on a rock—twenty or thirty feet above the road—where we were riding.
> I called out, "What are you doing there?"
> "I'm watching Life," he said.
> "Is that all?" said my companion.
> "Young man, isn't that enough?" said he. "Could you do better? I am extremely busy. I have spoken."
> Then he spoke no more. . . . I was thrilled through and through.[11]

In the midst of polishing *The Madman* to present to a publisher, Kahlil was also painting furiously for a December exhibition at the

Montross Gallery on Fifth Avenue, a rare opportunity. Yet he felt a new phase of life was awaiting him. He wrote to Mary:

> Early tomorrow morning I must help hang the pictures. In the afternoon there will be a crowd. Everybody wants to know if I am to be there. Perhaps I shall have to be there for an hour or so. But I shall not go again! I have finished those pictures and I am finished with them. They belong to the past. My whole being is directed towards a fresh start. This exhibition is the end of a chapter.[12]

Most encouraging to Kahlil at this exhibition was the presence of the reclusive sixty-seven-year-old American painter Albert Pinkham Ryder. Ryder was an eccentric best known for his poetic and metaphorical work and seascapes, and Kahlil admired his work and longed to meet him. The previous April he had written to Mary:

> The big person in this country is Ryder. There is so much in what he has done. The man is the great thing. He's very hard to see.[13]

Through some creative networking, Kahlil sent Ryder a prose poem written in his honor as a thank-you for taking time to see the work of a younger artist; this led to an opportunity of Ryder sitting for a portrait by Kahlil. Kahlil also mailed copies of this poetic tribute he had written in English to some of his friends. The rector of the nearby Episcopal church on West 10th Street, Church of the Ascension, even read it from his pulpit one day.

During the years of the First World War, Kahlil became active in raising relief funds to assist those starving from the famine and suffering resulting from the destitution that had befallen Lebanon. He also began hosting a weekly gathering of Arab literary friends, which they called "Arrabitah" (The Pen Bond), providing an opportunity for younger writers to discuss modern Arabic literature. The group became a prominent proponent of the Arab literary Romanticism movement. His lifelong friend Mischa, who would be his first biographer, arrived in the autumn of 1916 to join the young Arabic literary movement in New York. Later, Mischa and Ameen Rihani both became known for their significant contributions to the developing of *Mahjar*, the Arab immigrant literature movement.

The Madman, the first of what would be called Kahlil's "little black books" to appear in English, was published in 1918 by Alfred A. Knopf, founder of a new publishing house in New York City. In recognizing the appeal of Kahlil's aphoristic style, its publication inaugurated a new literary career for Kahlil, and he began drawing attention in the literary world. The Poetry Society of America read two of the longer pieces in *The Madman*, which led to a new admirer, Corinne Roosevelt Robinson, a sister of former president Theodore Roosevelt. This in turn led to Kahlil attending and participating numerous times in poetry readings she held in her home.

As previously seen in the short story "Yuhanna the Mad," the theme of madness resurfaces in *The Madman*, albeit this time with a new purposeful force. Kahlil portrays madness metaphorically, like a veil of protection as a result of not being understood on a deeper spiritual level. This veil of sorts can also be seen in many of his drawings, which are cloaked in mystery, subjects frequently with eyes closed, symbolizing spiritual blindness or the invitation to look beyond the superficial layer of life. Sometimes his artworks continue off the page, conveying in an imaginative sense that the full story lies beyond the surface of apparent vision. When someone asked him, "What is a mystic?" Kahlil is said to have smiled and replied, "Nothing very secret nor formidable—just someone who has drawn aside *one more veil*."[14]

In a letter to Mischa in 1921 he wrote:

> I say that madness is the first step towards divine sublimation. Be mad, Mischa. Be mad and tell us of the mysteries behind the veil of "reason." Life's purpose is to bring us nearer to those mysteries; and madness is the surest and the quickest steed. Be mad, and remain a mad brother to your mad brother.[15]
>
> Spiritual freedom comes from within, never from without.[16]

As I looked at the many books that made up Kahlil's library, now all on display at the Gibran Museum in Bsharri, Lebanon, it was clear that he remained fascinated with the theme of madness and its spiritual imagery. On the shelves were Fyodor Dostoevsky's classic *The Idiot*, Leo Tolstoy's *The Story of Ivan the Fool* and *Memoirs of a Madman*, Cervantes's *Don Quixote*, and works of the great Russian authors Pushkin, Chekhov, Turgenev, and Bulgakov, all of whom explore the theme of madness in their writings.

Prince Vladimir Odoevsky's great work of essays and novellas, *Russian Nights*, sits prominently on one of the shelves, containing that provocative query about "insanity."

> Isn't the exalted state of a poet, or an inventor, closer to what is called insanity than insanity is to an ordinary animal-like stupidity? Isn't what we call common sense a highly elastic term, a term used by an ordinary person against a great man who is incomprehensible to him, and also by a man of genius to cover up his reasonings and not to frighten an ordinary person with them?[17]

Kahlil owned numerous books on William Blake, whom he saw as his mentor through his art and poetry. One book in particular that I picked up and opened, *The Art of William Blake*, was obviously gifted to him, inscribed on the title page, "To Kahlil Gibran, 1926." A passion for the "heart of the matter," and living from within, is infused into all Kahlil's work, reminiscent of Blake, yet whose work is more apocalyptic in nature than Kahlil's.

> I shall be happy when men shall say about me what they said of Blake: "He is a madman." Madness in art is creation. Madness in poetry is wisdom. Madness in the search for God is the highest form of worship.[18]

Blake was widely seen by most as mad when he died in 1827. •The primary reasons for his being labeled "mad" were the bizarre visions he received and his habit of speaking quite naturally of spiritual visitors. Blake would offhandedly mention in a conversation that he had been speaking to Milton, or another dead poet or king. And he said he experienced romantic visions, such as sculptures of sheep in the middle of a field.

Blake actually had these visions as a child. When he was four years of age, while playing he claimed to have seen God put his head up against the window to look at him. A few years later he saw angels perched on the limbs of a tree. He never outgrew these visions, and they inspired him to spiritual and artistic heights. Hence his work is seen as esoteric and mysterious; he claimed to see things in the spiritual world and painted what he saw.

Following Blake's death, his first biographer, Alexander Gilchrist, dedicated a whole chapter of his *Life of William Blake* to this theme, titling it "Mad or Not Mad." As he looks at Blake's life and work, he redeems Blake's reputation in defining the "special faculty" of his imagination and defends his spiritual sanity, attributing Blake's visions to the peculiar power of a mystical and creative genius, a power of which he was in full control. Echoing Kahlil's view on those considered mad, Gilchrist praises Blake's creativity by asking, "Does not prophet or hero always seem 'mad' to the respectable mob, and to polished men of the world?"[19]

The great early-twentieth-century English writer and humorist G. K. Chesterton came to a similar conclusion in his excellent biography of Blake. Chesterton directly addresses whether Blake's genius was clouded by madness or whether his unique vision on the world was the secret of his spiritual and artistic success. One of my own mentors, Malcolm Muggeridge, like Kahlil, saw sanity in Blake's madness. In his book taken from his BBC television series *The Third Testament*, Muggeridge shares his spiritual admiration for Blake:

> Blake's work is, to me, one of the great expressions of sanity that exist. Nor does it in the least surprise me that, for this very reason, he was in his time considered mad, and would today certainly be subjected to psychiatric treatment, with a view to drugging or psychoanalyzing and shocking him into what passes for sanity. . . . The faculty whereby Blake saw into the reality of things he called Imagination, and this is what he remained true to, from the beginning to the end. . . . In the end Blake came to see that the only true freedom is spiritual, achieved through the imagination. . . . Was Blake in this sense mad? . . . Mad? I should say sane to the point of sublimity.[20]

Kahlil's fascination with madness reminds me of another English writer, Colin Wilson, whose first book, *The Outsider*, published in 1952, I found profoundly revelatory. Wilson, a twenty-four-year-old homeless writer at the time, wrote the book in the Reading Room of the British Museum. He explores the whole concept of "the outsider," of "human alienation" in society, by looking at the lives and works of numerous great artists, such as H. G. Wells, Franz Kafka, Albert Camus, Jean-Paul Sartre, T. S. Eliot, Ernest Hemingway, Hermann Hesse, T. E. Lawrence, Vincent van Gogh, George Bernard Shaw, William Blake, Friedrich Nietzsche, and G. I. Gurdjieff. I have run into numerous people who feel it is still one of the most important books they have read.

The theme of madness, whether real or perceived, intrigued Kahlil. He often portrayed the madman as saner than others, forcing readers to look beyond superficial assumptions. In *The Madman*, Kahlil introduces his series of short parables and reflections based on Lebanese folklore by describing a madman who has been freed from the masks of life that were binding his soul.

> Thus I became a madman. And I have found both freedom and safety in my madness; the freedom of loneliness and the safety from being understood, for those who understand us enslave something in us.[21]

"God," the first prose poem in *The Madman*, reflects Kahlil's belief in the omnipresence of the Divine. It is about a seeker who climbs the holy mountain promising devotion, servitude, and obedience to God but receives no answer. In an obvious allusion to that seemingly crazed biblical prophet Elijah's experience with God on the mountain, God first passes by like "a mighty tempest," then like "a thousand swift wings," and then like "the mist that veils the distant hills." The seeker's last attempt addresses God not as an unreachable being but as an integral part of the sacred order of life:

> And after a thousand years I climbed the sacred mountain and again spoke unto God, saying, "My God, my aim and my fulfillment; I am thy yesterday and thou art my tomorrow. I am thy

root in the earth and thou art my flower in the sky, and together we grow before the face of the sun."

Then God leaned over to me, and in my ears whispered words of sweetness, and even as the sea that enfoldeth a brook that runneth down to her, he enfolded me.

And when I descended to the valleys and the plains God was there also.[22]

One of Kahlil's most moving drawings in the book accompanies his reflection titled "War." It is a depiction of the Crucifixion with Jesus's arms freely stretched out to touch the whole world in a sign of empathy and blessing. While the world's religions are visibly represented by intertwined figures, the people themselves are pictured as bent, twisted, and trapped under the weight of the world's oppression.[23]

In contrast to Kahlil's writings that precede *The Madman*, there is a definite reordering of his orientation from being primarily against the "wrongs of the world" toward an invitation to contemplation, harmony, and spirituality. His poems and parables are meant to stir reflective questioning. In his parable "The Good God and the Evil God," he imaginatively makes his point, addressing the absurdity of common misperceptions on the spiritual realities of our world.

The Good God and the Evil God met on the mountain top.

The Good God said, "Good day to you, brother."

The Evil God made no answer.

And the Good God said, "You are in a bad humour today."

"Yes," said the Evil God, "for of late I have been often mistaken for you, called by your name, and treated as if I were you, and it ill-pleases me."

And the Good God said, "But I too have been mistaken for you and called by your name."

The Evil God walked away cursing the stupidity of man.[24]

However, perhaps of all the stories in *The Madman*, the one that most clearly illustrates Kahlil's view of "madness" as seeing beyond the veil, seeing what others don't see, is called "The Eye." It is one of my favorites in this collection, and its profound simplicity sums up the heart of Kahlil's understanding in seeing the deepest dimension of spiritual reality.

> Said the Eye one day, "I see beyond these valleys a mountain veiled with blue mist. Is it not beautiful?"
>
> The Ear listened, and after listening intently awhile, said, "But where is any mountain? I do not hear it."
>
> Then the Hand spoke and said, "I am trying in vain to feel it or touch it, and I can find no mountain."
>
> And the Nose said, "There is no mountain, I cannot smell it."
>
> Then the Eye turned the other way, and they all began to talk together about the Eye's strange delusion. And they said, "Something must be the matter with the Eye."[25]

The Tempest   5

I shall be a tempest in their sky, and a song in their soul.

—KAHLIL GIBRAN, *JESUS THE SON OF MAN*[1]

I HAVE ALWAYS BEEN FASCINATED BY STORMS. As a child growing up in Senegal, we had storms called the Harmattan. The storms would come in off the Sahara Desert down into the Sahel to the West African coast. Picking up sand along the way, by the time they reached us they were full of fine red clay dust that filled the air.

The winds that propel these storms increase the threat of bush fires and can cause severe crop damage. When the Harmattan trade winds interacted with southerly monsoon rains, the storms that ensued would be calamitous, tearing apart the poorly built housing structures in rural West Africa. As a young boy, I remember the Harmattan haze that would set in, and could block the sun for several days, like a heavy, dry, dusty fog. It costs airlines in the region millions of dollars each year to cancel and divert flights.

Living in Egypt we had the *Khamaseen* sandstorms, their name derived from the Arabic word for "fifty." These spring storms would whip up sporadically over about a fifty-day period, carrying in fine dust off the desert that would penetrate our windows and leave an almost sticky residue on our tables. We would all hunker down when these winds blew because there was no escaping grit in your hair, eyes, ears, mouth, and nose if you were caught outside. During these storms Cairo in effect closed down, as most sought refuge inside.

Stories still circulate that both Napoleon's military campaigns in Egypt as well as Allied and German forces in North Africa during the Second World War faced these dreaded *Khamaseens*. They were forced to halt fighting when sand whirled, temporarily blinding soldiers and creating electrical disturbances that could render compasses useless.

One year in Egypt we lived through a locust swarm, a storm like I'd never before experienced. News had spread in advance that swarms were moving toward Cairo. Our children were off at school the day the locusts arrived and, we hoped, safely indoors. When the skies eerily darkened and the locusts swept through our neighborhood, it felt as though an ancient plague was descending upon us. Many locusts fell to the earth as massive swarms ripped through the city, and our kids enthusiastically reported afterward that their science teachers had let them collect specimens for research purposes.

Some of the rainstorms I remember most clearly were in tropical Africa, when I was working briefly in Matadi, Congo's main port on the left bank of the great Congo River. The forest rainstorms pounded so heavily on the corrugated tin roofs that you could not hear the person next to you speaking. The skies opened up and literally everything shut down, including electricity, so everyone took shelter inside in the dark. We became hermits in the storm. I recall standing in awe at the power of the thrashing storm as it raged on and on.

Kahlil felt these kinds of connections to the power of storms—the tempests, as he often called them. And as he did not separate the material world from the spiritual, he saw life as a tempest and learned the beauty of embracing it.

Yet the years after the First World War weighed heavily on Kahlil. He struggled with health issues as a result of many hardships and an unhealthy lifestyle: smoking, heavy coffee drinking, skipping meals, drinking arak (the strong anise-based Middle Eastern liquor), and often working obsessively all through the night. He had left the land of his childhood; lost his mother, brother, and sister within an eighteen-month period; and his pursuit of love was fraught with disappointment. Just the distress of leaving his childhood roots in rural Lebanon to settle into urban industrialization in one of poorest sections of Boston would have been enough to cause ongoing internal upheaval. Although much of his art over the years explored the realms of Symbolist Romanticism, Kahlil also did portrait work and family scenes, but his portrayals of families, children, and mothers often showed signs of distress.

The many personal losses he had experienced began to layer, causing waves of anxiety, grief, and depression. Kahlil's father died while he was studying in Paris, although it was reported that his father had blessed him on his deathbed, after a lifetime of disapproval. In addition he suffered major financial losses due to failed business dealings. As the storms of life threatened to overwhelm him, Kahlil chose to explore the tempest metaphor, a theme he often revisited throughout his life. In *The Madman*, he expressed his inner struggles, reflecting the tension of being caught between two cultures.

> But why should I be here, O God, I a green seed of unfulfilled passion, a mad tempest that seeketh neither east nor west, a bewildered fragment from a burnt planet?[2]

By the time the First World War was officially under way Kahlil's homeland of Lebanon had already suffered greatly under the Turks, causing intense emotional angst for Kahlil. He sought ways to turn his feelings of helplessness into more tangible expressions and continued to pour himself into his art and writing. In great celebration at the war's end in November 1918 he wrote to Mary Haskell:

> Out of the dark mist a new world is born. It is indeed a holy day. The most holy since the birth of Jesus. The air is crowded with

the sound of rushing waters and the beating of Mighty Wings. The voice of God is in the wind.[3]

When I visited the Soumaya Museum in Mexico City, I saw a handwritten letter that Kahlil's friend Barbara Young had written to his sister Marianna, expressing how relieved she was that Kahlil did not have to live through the Second World War as well.

> I have thought often how glad I am that Kahlil did not stay here to behold this ghastly horror and nightmare that has befallen the planet. His agony would have been intolerable.[4]

The theme of suffering and death weighed heavily on Kahlil. I remember seeing one of his drawings from 1910 in the Telfair Museum of Art in Savannah, Georgia, depicting a reminder that death is always present. It is a charcoal drawing of a beautiful woman in the forefront with a skull floating in the air behind her. The museum labeled it "Woman and Death's Head," but Kahlil had left it untitled.

After the end of the First World War, the following year of 1919 saw the publication in English of a book of Kahlil's drawings titled *Twenty Drawings*. He also published a long prose poem written in classical Arabic called *The Processions*, a dialogue between a spiritually awakened man and a man in bondage. As these thoughts were materializing, he was also hard at work on a collection of prose and short stories called *The Tempests*.

The Tempests was published in Arabic in Cairo in 1920, and it gives us a deeper glimpse into his fascination with storms that developed when he was a young boy in Lebanon. He loved the power and wonder they evoked. Mary records Kahlil's enchantment with storms in her journal after a visit together during the summer of 1920:

> A big storm broke, with torrents of rain and with thunder. Kahlil was elated. "Mary, a storm does something for me that nothing else on earth does. In a storm like this one I rode on a white horse at a run, galloped fifteen or sixteen miles. The horse was

probably a little bit maddened. I was exceedingly happy. My first memory is of a storm. I tore my clothes to run out into it. They ran after me, and brought me back. I was soaked and they rubbed me with alcohol. But I ran out into many another. Everything I've done that is biggest has come from a storm. My latest book is named *Storms* (*The Tempests*)." There came a great thunder roll. "That went through me like Christ speaking to me," said Kahlil.[5]

One of Kahlil's stories that I find especially thought-provoking is the pinnacle piece in *The Tempests*. It is a short story called "The Tempest," placed in the setting of his childhood, the Qadisha Valley, about a young man who is roaming the cedar forests one autumn afternoon and gets caught in a terrible rainstorm. He seeks cover in an isolated shelter inhabited by a hermit, Yusif El Fakhri, someone he had heard of from local villagers and had longed to meet one day.

Kahlil decorated his home studio "hermitage" sparsely in a manner that created a contemplative atmosphere. A simple wooden bed, several crucifixes made of wood and metal, a small brass chalice, an easel, and a tapestry of an Eastern Christ hung on the wall above an altar-like table with brass candlesticks. It was a reminder to him of the hermitage near where he had spent his childhood in Lebanon. Five years before his death, he had considered purchasing the Carmelite monastery for his retirement and its monks' hermitage for his final repose. His dream did materialize following his death, as his will requested that he be buried in the grotto of that same hermitage in what is today the Gibran Museum in Bsharri.

In Kahlil's day, while some believed that hermits were mystics, most assumed they were madmen. It is rare for a person to withdraw from society into isolation in the context of a Middle Eastern communal culture, such as exists in Lebanon. When living in Egypt, it was fascinating to see how even life in prison is lived in community. I remember going to visit a Belgian in prison in Cairo who had been arrested for selling drugs. The prisoner's mother had asked me to visit him, as he was allowed to receive visitors, but she could only come from Belgium several times a year. On my first visit I imagined him being held in isolation, locked up in an individual cell. But to my surprise, he was in one large room with all the other prisoners. I was not allowed to enter that area of the prison, but I learned that the inmates naturally divided themselves into communities based on where they were from in Egypt. As he was the only foreigner, he had to join a community for safety and food. He had changed "communities" several times in the years he had been there. Families would send food regularly to the prison, and the prisoners helped provide for one another. Tora Prison, where he was being held, was just a couple miles from where we lived. It was also known as Egypt's political prison; hence, during the 2011 Egyptian Revolution, it was one of the prisons attacked during the days of chaos, and many of those who were imprisoned there by President Mubarak were set free.

My first visit in Egypt to the oldest monastery in the world, St. Anthony's near the Red Sea, was a powerful experience. At that time the many ancient frescoes in the church were being restored. For centuries they had not been visible due to accumulated dirt, smoke damage from candles and incense, as well as layers of graffiti, including from the hands of historic Crusaders passing through the region. All of this was slowly being removed, and the frescoes beneath were breathtaking. Vivid in color, they were being restored to their original beauty.

St. Anthony was a fourth-century Middle Eastern monk in Egypt who gave birth to the idea of monastic life. Anthony settled into a small cave—a hermitage—secluded on the edge of a barren rocky cliff near the Red Sea. Pilgrims today still make the climb up to his dwelling. The first time I visited St. Anthony's, I had imagined meeting quiet ascetics steeped in meditation and withdrawn from society. Instead I found a vibrant community of active monastics. The monastery guide was a resident monk who wore the traditional long black Coptic Orthodox robe with a camel-leather Coptic cross hanging from his neck and embroidered crosses on his skullcap. In the midst of his overview to visitors about the monastery's history, we heard the incongruous sound of a cell phone ringing. Moments later our monk rummaged through his long flowing robe and pulled out a black flip phone. Before that conversation had ended, another phone began ringing; he sheepishly smiled at us and dug out a second cell phone from his other deep pocket. Reflecting the communal nature of Middle Eastern culture, as opposed to being cloistered, we found the monks of St. Anthony's to be vital members of the Coptic Orthodox Church at large, running church publishing companies and charities and actively leading spiritual retreats.

We did learn that there was a separate area of the monastery designated for reflective respite when desired, and communal prayers were woven into the routines of their days and nights. Although the hermitage Kahlil would have encountered in Lebanon as a child was nestled into a forest of trees rather than barren desert, the cultural workings of its monastic life were probably very similar. The imagery of monastic life was something Kahlil admired.

My first experience within the walls of a Middle Eastern monastery took place before I moved to Egypt. I had been invited to speak at a spiritual retreat at the fourth-century Coptic monastery of St. Bishoy in the Wadi El Natrun, a desert valley in the Nitrian Desert. All I knew of the Wadi El Natrun was through the writings of the French writer and aviator Antoine de Saint-Exupéry, who crashed his airplane in the desert there, survived, and went on to write his famous philosophical novella *The Little Prince*, highlighting the metaphysical insights he gained from his experience of being marooned in the area's barrenness. I soon learned that this ancient monastery named for the Desert Father St. Bishoy had more recently been a prison of sorts for the late Pope Shenouda III, the head of the Coptic Orthodox Church, who was kept there under house arrest during the years Anwar Sadat was president of Egypt. It was indeed a fascinating place, with ancient churches, cells for monks, refectories, a four-story modern "palace," and relics of Coptic saints, including the purported incorruptible body of St. Bishoy himself. I also discovered that Pope Shenouda III kept a zoo of exotic animals in his private monastery quarters, which I thoroughly enjoyed walking through in the coolness of the early mornings. Yet despite the many inspiring experiences I have had there since, I will never forget the mosquitoes. On my first night I climbed onto my rock-hard mattress and glanced up at the tall arched ceiling before turning out my light. A dark mass of mosquitoes loomed high above. I crawled under the sheets, turned off the light, and waited. Minutes later I flipped on the light switch and looked up at the ceiling; there was not a mosquito in sight, as all were already on their way down toward me. At breakfast the next morning, I noticed the swollen, red-marked faces of the other priests. No one had been spared.

In Kahlil's story "The Tempest," our first-person narrator realizes that the storm is a fortunate opportunity, as he has long wanted to learn this old hermit's spiritual secrets.

> I was in a miserable plight when I reached the hermitage, and as I knocked on the door the man whom I had been longing to see opened it. He was holding in one hand a dying bird whose head had been injured and whose wings had been broken.[6]

Upon being let in, the elderly hermit Yusif says to the story's narrator, when he complains about the tempest outside:

> The tempest is clean . . . why do you seek to escape from it? . . . The tempest would have bestowed upon you a great honour . . . if she had swallowed you.[7]

As the old man gently attends to the bird's injuries he says:

> It is my wish that man would show the bird's instinct . . . for man inclines towards fear . . . and as he feels the awakening of the tempest he crawls into the crevices and the caves of the earth and hides himself.[8]
>
> Many are those who lift their heads above the mountain tops, but their spirits remain dormant in the obscurity of the caverns.[9]

Referencing biblical imagery, Yusif continues:

I came to this place when the earth was without form, and void; and darkness was upon the face of the deep. And the Spirit of God moved upon the face of the waters.[10]

The hour begins to get late:

Night was spreading her black garment upon those valleys, and the tempest was shrieking dizzily and the rain becoming stronger. I began to fancy that the Biblical flood was coming again.[11]

The old man engages in conversation reluctantly and slowly imparts his wisdom through beautiful imagery. Again, we see the weaving of seasons into Kahlil's writing.

I sought solitude for in it there is a full life for the spirit and for the heart and for the body. I found the endless prairies where the light of the sun rests, and where the flowers breathe their fragrance into space, and where the streams sing their way to the sea. I discovered the mountains where I found the fresh awakening of Spring, and the colourful longing of Summer, and the rich songs of Autumn, and the beautiful mystery of Winter. I came to this far corner of God's domain for I hungered to learn the secrets of the Universe, and approach close to the throne of God.[12]

The theme of the spirit's awakening emerges as conversation continues:

And among all vanities of life, there is only one thing that the spirit loves and craves. . . . It is an awakening in the spirit; it is an awakening in the inner depths of the heart; it is an overwhelming and magnificent power that descends suddenly upon man's conscience and opens his eyes, whereupon he sees Life amid a dizzying shower of brilliant music, surrounded by a circle of great light, with man standing as a pillar of beauty between the earth and the firmament. . . . It is a secret hand which removed the veil from my eyes.[13]

Yusif, the old sage, bared his soul, clarifying that he left the world to "live in the awakeness of life" and "think upon the compelling and beautiful mystery of existence."[14]

Thinking of the tempest of life, I am reminded of a poignant novel titled *Ports of Call*, written by the renowned Lebanese-French writer Amin Maalouf, whom many see as reflecting the spirit of Kahlil Gibran today. I was so moved by the story that I sought out Maalouf in Paris to secure the film rights to the book. At that time I had hoped that legendary Egyptian actor Omar Sharif, a friend, who had previously acted the role of Kahlil Gibran in film and was a fan of Maalouf's writings, would play a role in the eventual production of the movie. *Ports of Call* tells the story of a man going through a tremendous tempest in his life. It is an epic love story between a Lebanese-Turkish Muslim man, Ossyane, whose mother was Armenian Christian, and a Jewish woman, Clara, whom he met when serving in the French Resistance during the Second World War. Ossyane lived a virtual tempest in terms of both the love and the life he lost due to the many years he was unjustly locked away in a Lebanese asylum. In many ways the story is a microcosm of the Middle East, a turbulent and war-torn region. Addressing the inordinate amount of innocent suffering experienced due to ethnic, religious, and national conflicts, the story nevertheless profoundly contributes to overcoming traditional prejudices with respect to the differences that have divided people and made them enemies.

When I went to Paris to meet Amin Maalouf, we had dinner together and talked until well after midnight over two bottles of champagne, his drink of choice. The aspect of *Ports of Call*'s story that spoke most powerfully to me was the sense that Ossyane, who narrates the story as an older man, had lived an incredibly difficult life but had overcome its power to destroy his spirit. He had learned to embrace the storm. The hardships he experienced were beyond his control, but through them all his true spirit emerged, resilient and beautiful. After a quarter of a century, the lovers' reunion at the end of the book is one of the most moving passages I have ever read. Ossyane had come through and overcome the tempest. Maalouf, in one of his other novels, expresses thanks to God for life's "storms."

Let us thank God for having made us this gift of death, so that
life is to have meaning; of night, that day is to have meaning;
silence, that speech is to have meaning; illness, that health is to
have meaning; war, that peace is to have meaning. Let us give
thanks to Him for having given us weariness and pain, so that rest
and joy are to have meaning. Let us give thanks to him, whose
wisdom is infinite.[15]

At the powerful conclusion of "The Tempest," the old hermit
Yusif leaves the young man sheltered in his hermitage.

I am going now to walk through the night with the tempest. . . it
is a practice that I enjoy greatly. . . . I hope you will teach yourself
to love, and not to fear, the tempest.[16]

Kahlil's ability to face life's storms, rather than run from them,
liberated him internally, and through his writings he sought to
share this freedom with others. In thinking of Kahlil's life, I am
reminded of the wise words of Origen, the third-century church
father from Egypt: "You have coals of fire . . . sit on them and
they will be of help to you."[17] Kahlil continued to journey, to
grow, and to learn from the storms of life. In a letter to May in
Cairo some years later, he wrote: "If you only knew how much I
need simplicity. I wish you knew how much I long for the absolute . . . the absolute in the storm."[18]

I saw a fascinating painting by Kahlil at the Gibran Museum
in Bsharri called *Tempest Rising in the Spirit of the Poet*. It is a dark
painting with a storm brewing. A man alone with a walking stick
is slumped over. One thing that struck me in the Gibran Museum
was how many of his paintings are related to this theme. There is
a very emotive work called *Anguish*. Just a few feet away is another
poignant work, titled *On Death and Despair*. Clearly, Kahlil was
captivated with the tempests of life, both spiritual and physical.

As I wandered through the museum, I was drawn to an early
handwritten draft of Kahlil's final book, *Jesus the Son of Man*. I was
struck by how Kahlil described Jesus's death through the voice of

Mary Magdalene: "On that day there was a great storm that swept the valley."

Another story in this collection published with "The Tempest" was one that Kahlil wrote on Good Friday called "The Crucified," in which he portrayed Jesus with the strength of a raging tempest.

> The Nazarene was not weak! He was strong and is strong! But the people refuse to heed the true meaning of strength. . . . Jesus was not a bird with broken wings; He was a raging tempest who broke all crooked wings.[19]

In a letter to May in Cairo, apparently addressing a concern she had about *The Tempests*, he wrote:

> What am I to say about the caverns of my soul? Those caverns that frighten you so—I take refuge there when I grow weary of the ways of men, of their rankly blossoming fields and overgrown forests. I retreat into the caverns of my soul when I can find no other place to rest my head; and if some of those whom I love possessed the courage to enter into these caverns they would find nothing but a man on his knees saying his prayers.[20]

In *The Tempests*, the theme of awakening continues to evolve in Kahlil's story titled "Eventide of the Feast." It is a dreamlike story that tells of a man portrayed as homeless and a bit mad who asks another man for shelter. The man is willing to give him money for lodging at an inn, but he replies that he is not seeking a roof but human shelter. Eventually the man sees the marks of nails in his palms and cries out "Oh Jesus, the Nazarene!" He then awakes, realizing he had been dreaming.

> At that moment, I opened my eyes, lifted my head, and looked around, but found naught except a column of smoke before me, and I heard only the shivering voice of the silence of the night, coming from the depths of Eternity. I collected myself and looked again to the singing throngs in the distance, and a voice within me said, "The very strength that protects the heart from injury is the strength that prevents the heart from enlarging to its

intended greatness within. The song of the voice is sweet, but the song of the heart is the pure voice of heaven."[21]

I made a trip to Washington, DC, to see the Kahlil Gibran Memorial Garden, which was dedicated in 1991 by President George H. W. Bush. It was to be a quick trip because I was expected in New York for meetings; I decided to fly into Washington on my way and then take a train up to New York the following day. I woke up extremely early the day I was leaving to a torrential downpour. I was staying in a hotel across the Potomac River and could hear the relentless wind and rain driving sideways into my windowpane. I doubted my umbrella was going to be of much help. It was still early dawn when my prearranged chauffeur arrived to take me to Union Station via the memorial garden. My chauffeur was quick to inform me that he had just dropped off William Bennett, the former secretary of education, for his morning radio program. Evidently he drove him to the radio station each day. My driver was an older Sudanese Muslim, and his gracious spirit was contagious. When I told him we were going to the Gibran Memorial because I was writing a book about Kahlil, he immediately came to life, exclaiming, "Gibran is the answer to our needs today." He then went on to tell me that Ralph Nader, the political activist, attorney, and five-time presidential candidate, also of Lebanese descent, is related to Kahlil and that he had driven for him several times as well.

The memorial garden is located on Washington, DC's Embassy Row, directly across from the British Embassy and not far from the National Cathedral, the Islamic Center, a Jewish temple, and Orthodox churches. It is a very apropos setting for one who resonated with the great unity of life and wrote:

> Would that I could be the peacemaker in your soul, that I might turn the discord and the rivalry of your elements into oneness and melody.[22]

Aptly, I was making this journey in the middle of a raging storm, thinking of Kahlil's love of storms and the imagery found in "The

Tempest." Once I arrived at the memorial and started wandering around, holding on to my flimsy umbrella, I came across a thoughtful line of Kahlil's etched in marble: "Do not the spirits who dwell in the ether envy man his pain?" Kahlil believed that in order to be fully alive one had to embrace life's storms that whirled with pain and to view life's suffering as a gift to be experienced.

The same year that *The Tempests* was released in Arabic, Kahlil's *The Forerunner* was published in English. It has a very different feel than his previous work. Kahlil is much more settled and mature, less self-introspective and more outwardly focused on others. His same depth and life values shine through, but the cynicism and sense of despair had lessened. One piece, "Said a Sheet of Snow-White Paper," perhaps more clearly than anything else he wrote, illustrates Kahlil's embrace of the storms of life, subtly echoing *The Tempests'* voice:

> Said a sheet of snow-white paper, "Pure was I created, and pure will I remain for ever. I would rather be burnt and turn to white ashes than suffer darkness to touch me or the unclean to come near me." The ink-bottle heard what the paper was saying, and it laughed in its dark heart; but it never dared to approach her. And the multicolored pencils heard her also, and they too never came near her. And the snow-white sheet of paper did remain pure and chaste for ever—pure and chaste—and empty.[23]

The Prophet   6

The veil that clouds our eyes shall be lifted
by the hands that wove it,
And the clay that fills your ears shall be pierced
by the fingers that kneaded it.
And you shall see.
And you shall hear.

—KAHLIL GIBRAN, *THE PROPHET*[1]

ST. MARK'S CHURCH-IN-THE-BOWERY in Manhattan's
East Village is the oldest site of continuous religious practice
in New York. Starting in the early 1900s under the dynamic
leadership of its minister, Reverend William Norman Guthrie, a close friend of architect Frank Lloyd Wright, this historic
church become known for focusing on faith and the arts, hosting numerous artists, writers, poets, actors, and dancers. Pulitzer
Prize–winning poet Carl Sandburg, modernist poet William Carlos Williams, dancers Isadora Duncan and Martha Graham, and
the great Harry Houdini himself all performed at this imaginative
church. St. Mark's also became a beacon for those creatively pushing the boundaries of traditional Christian beliefs and exploring
Eastern spirituality.

Sitting on a park bench on a scorching summer afternoon in front of this ecclesiastical icon of creativity and unorthodoxy, I couldn't think of a more fitting place for Kahlil's best-selling book, *The Prophet*, to have been launched in 1923. No wonder Kahlil spoke so appreciatively of this church, whose minister he admired. There he gave readings of his work and held an exhibition of his drawings. Reverend Guthrie first heard Kahlil read his work at a Poetry Society event in 1919 and invited him to display a collection of his drawings at the church. Flipping through a first edition copy of *The Prophet* that I was carrying with me, generously given to me by my sister, I noticed it was printed in 1940, albeit in the original publication format. I sat there savoring the thought that this book in my hands was remarkably its thirty-eighth print run in just seventeen years.

Mystical, spiritual, philosophical, twenty-eight poetic reflections and barely twenty thousand words in length, *The Prophet*, known as the "little black book," was an unlikely bestseller whose influence rapidly spread from the streets of New York City to the world beyond. Within a month, all thirteen hundred copies of the first print run had been sold.[2] St. Mark's Church-in-the-Bowery hosted the first public reading of *The Prophet*, and it was standing room only to hear it read by Butler Davenport, a well-known actor of the time. Kahlil attended this first public reading and commented afterward:

> To my regret he read the whole book . . . but his spirit was ever so good. . . . I had wanted it first read in a church.[3]

Kahlil's soon-to-be friend Barbara Young happened to be present at that first public reading and wrote of the experience:

> [I]t was not by chance that when *The Prophet* was read for the first time in public, at St. Mark's In-the-Bouwrie in New York City on an autumn afternoon in 1923, I sat in the crowded church and listened to the reading by Butler Davenport, that distinguished gentleman of the theatre. I knew only that I had heard startling and essential truth spoken with a power and a beauty that I had never heard or read anywhere up to that moment. It was inevi-

table that I should have a copy of the book for my own, and that I should share it immediately with others, many others.[4]

The publication of *The Prophet* burst onto the scene as the world was still reeling from the First World War, some working tirelessly to rebuild as the economic and cultural boon of the Roaring Twenties emerged and others still trying to make sense of all the bloodshed. That year, the world at large witnessed the establishment of the Soviet Union, Lenin's call for Stalin's removal, the Turkish War of Independence ending the Ottoman Empire, Hitler inciting hatred in Berlin, Mussolini's invasion of Corfu, mass arrests of Mafia members in America, and active warnings against the actions of the Ku Klux Klan. On a lighter note, Howard Carter, funded by Lord Carnarvon in England, discovered Pharaoh Tutankhamun's grave, *Time* magazine debuted, transcontinental airmail service began, inflatable tires appeared on the market, traffic signals and the electric razor were invented, the Walt Disney Company was founded, and Houdini freed himself from a straitjacket while suspended upside-down forty feet above the ground in New York City.

Twenty years in the making, *The Prophet* was a project Kahlil revisited again and again, waiting patiently for its form and then its content to take shape into something worthy of sharing. The year before it was published, Mary Haskell recorded in her journal time spent with Kahlil on the line-spacing of what they were then going to call the "Counsels." Interestingly, Mary used this working title in referring to it even after it was published. Each of the "Counsels" expressed words of wisdom, and Kahlil summed up the book's theme in a letter to Mary that same month:

> The whole Prophet is saying just one thing:
> "you are far far greater than you know—and All is well."[5]

The *Chicago Evening Post* wrote of *The Prophet*:

> The rhythm of Gibran's words are retained in our ears like the majestic book "Ecclesiastes." Kahlil Gibran is not afraid to be an idealist in an era abounding with cynicism. The twenty-eight

chapters of this little bible are recommended reading to those who are more than ever ready to see the truth.[6]

Kahlil's friend Mischa, also a Lebanese immigrant to America, reflected on *The Prophet*:

For Gibran knew how to make of it a perfect plant with roots buried deep in the soil of human life thus assuring it of constant sustenance. So long as men experience birth and death; so long as they eat and drink, love and hate, marry and beget children, laugh and weep; so long as men are men, just so long will they seek the meanings of birth and death, of love and hate and all the other relations that bind them to each other and to the nature about them, and who will find comfort in Gibran's interpretation of those relations.[7]

Later, during the distress of the Second World War, readership of *The Prophet* only increased, and by 1944 it was a bestseller, second only to the Pulitzer Prize–winning novel by John Hersey, *A Bell for Adano*. At a Fifth Avenue bookshop in New York, an elderly woman explained *The Prophet's* popularity: "I want this book. . . . Only . . . it isn't a book. It's bread and wine for tired people like me."[8] By 1957 it had been translated into twenty languages and a million copies had been sold; by 1970 it was selling, on average, about 7,000 copies a week, more than four million copies overall in America alone.[9]

Kahlil continued to reside in New York City at his "hermitage" studio apartment, and by the time *The Prophet* was published, it was evident that his spiritual journey was no longer just one man's search for meaning. Arising from his internalized bridging of the Eastern and Western influences of his life, a faith had emerged that transcended all cultures and religions. The roots of what he expresses in *The Prophet* were present in his earliest works, yet over time his voice became much more optimistic and self-confident.

While studying in Paris years earlier, Kahlil was introduced to an older man named Ameen Rihani, also a writer and of Maronite Christian background, and they became close friends. They both were born in Lebanon and were now living in the West, seeking to integrate their lives across cultures and express themselves through art and writing. Rihani had started out as an artist and was a great admirer of the poet William Blake. He eventually wrote what is considered to be the first novel written in English by an Arab-American, *The Book of Khalid*. It is largely autobiographical, and Kahlil designed an Arabesque illustration for its publication. Philosophical in nature, the hero of the story is a prophetic inspirational figure that perhaps served as an element of inspiration to Kahlil in his own writing of *The Prophet*.

Although Kahlil wrote *The Prophet* in English, its style reflects the majestic influence of his years spent writing in his mother tongue, Arabic. It carries the tone of a pensive Sufi mystic, a wise sage who has journeyed on ahead and now has wisdom to share. He did not confine himself to the writing styles of the day, in either Arabic or English, but, as with his art, let the words arise from within, unfettered and free. *The Prophet* is not solely philosophy, spiritual wisdom, or literature but an expression of Kahlil's own unique self, belonging not to East or West but to both. In harmony with the threads of mysticism in his work and life, he stands true to his own ideal. Kahlil wrote of the need for personal authenticity in an essay called "The Future of the Arabic Language."

> Let your national zeal spur you to depict the mysteries of pain and the miracles of joy that characterize life in the East, for it is better for you and for the Arabic language to adopt the simplest events in your surroundings and clothe them with the fabric of your imagination than to translate the most beautiful and the most respected of what the Westerners have written.[10]

Kahlil's words, spoken through his prophet, offer readers a time-less journey into the deeper dimensions of life, able to reach the soul of rural shepherd or intellectual academic alike. Stylistically, Nietzsche's book *Thus Spoke Zarathustra* was a work that Kahlil acknowledged as influential in his own journey and may have inspired him to respond, so to speak, by writing *The Prophet*. Where Nietzsche spread a threatening cloud of doom and gloom through his "discovery" that God is dead, a contrasting message is communicated in *The Prophet*. The similarities between the two books are striking, although their philosophical conclusions differ greatly. Zarathustra, Nietzsche's prophet, spends ten years in solitude in the Alps and then comes down the mountain to share his gleaned wisdom with the people below. Kahlil's prophet, Almustafa, on the other hand, waits twelve years for a ship to return and take him back to his home island. He comes down from his hill just before his ship leaves and addresses the people of Orphalese. Both speak to similar themes: freedom, crime, friendship, children, marriage, and death. Yet Kahlil con-tinually points readers to God, striving toward one's greater self and the aspiration of inclusivity, the embrace of all.

The Prophet was intended to be the first book in a trilogy Kahlil had planned. At the time of his death, he was working on the second book, *The Garden of the Prophet*, which was completed posthumously by his friend and assistant Barbara Young. Although the book does echo much of Kahlil's voice, it is hard to be sure exactly how much of it was really his own creation.

When *The Prophet* was published, Kahlil was facing serious finan-cial hardship, which Mary helped rectify, and he did not take much time to promote or savor the success of the book's reception, other than to speak at a banquet being hosted in his honor in Detroit.

I traveled to Detroit to see the Arab American Museum, a cul-tural museum highlighting those who are of Arab descent in the United States. Located in Dearborn, Michigan, where a high per-centage of the population is Arab, both Christian and Muslim, there are large churches of historic Middle Eastern Christian tradition in the area and quite striking mosques. I was struck by the beauty of the Arabesque architecture in the museum, with a traditional Arab courtyard of inlaid limestone, a mosaic tile floor, and an expansive calligraphic dome. However, after spending a few hours there, what most surprised me was how prominent Kahlil was in the museum and how important he is to Arab Americans. In addition to his profile on the wall of renowned Arab Americans, there is a model of the sculpture of Kahlil that is in the Gibran Memorial Garden in Washington, DC. And a special display case points to his influence on President John F. Kennedy's famous line in his inaugural address: "Ask not what your country can do for you." The resource library and bookstore are filled with Kahlil's books.

Fortuitously, a temporary exhibition at the museum by the late renowned Lebanese artist Sari Ibrahim Khoury beautifully mirrored what Kahlil was attempting to do in *The Prophet*. The museum emphasized how Khoury described his art as resulting from his "struggle between fragmentation and unity." And Khoury's work encompasses Arabic writing, Islamic design, and Byzantine Christian influences such as icons. Khoury, like Kahlil, sought to creatively highlight the necessity of a spirituality that embraces all and can be embraced by all.

Through the mouthpiece of Almustafa, whose name in Arabic means "the chosen one, the well-loved by God," Kahlil created a medium through *The Prophet* to invite others on a mystical journey through his spiritual poetic musings. Some of his messages are clear and some are nuanced, crafted with intention, expressing his developed spirituality. It is an invitation to greater depth in life, infused with a sense of wonder. Poetically woven throughout is a message of harmony and of hope, leading readers along what became his own spiritual path, beyond an interest in religion toward spiritual wholeness with God at the heart of life.

The narrative of *The Prophet* opens with words that set the tone for what is to unfold:

> Almustafa, the chosen and the beloved, who was a dawn unto his own day, had waited twelve years in the city of Orphalese for his ship that was to return and bear him back to the isle of his birth.[11]

Upon seeing the ship he has been longing for,

> the gates of his heart were flung open, and his joy flew far over the sea. And he closed his eyes and prayed in the silences of his soul.[12]

As he walks toward the ship, a group of admirers gather, along with the female seer Almitra, who intuitively realizes the significance of his departure and says:

> Prophet of God, in quest of the uttermost . . . disclose us to ourselves, and tell us all that has been shown you of that which is between birth and death.[13]

First she asks him to speak of Love. He answers,

> When love beckons to you, follow him,
> Though his ways are hard and steep.
> And when his wings enfold you yield to him,
> Though the sword hidden among his pinions may wound
>   you . . .
> he assigns you to his sacred fire, that you may become
>   sacred bread for God's sacred feast . . . that you may
>   know the secrets of your heart.[14]

He encourages them not to make the seeking of peace and pleasure their goal, as it would inhibit growth.

> Love possesses not nor would it be possessed; For love is sufficient unto love. When you love, you should not say, "God is in my heart," but rather, "I am in the heart of God." And think not you can direct the course of love, for love, if it finds you worthy, directs your course . . . let these be your desires: To melt and be

like a running brook that sings its melody to the night. . . . To wake at dawn with a winged heart and give thanks for another day of loving.[15]

The prose moves forward with musings on a variety of subjects—marriage, children, giving, eating and drinking.

A ploughman asks him to speak of Work:

And all work is empty save when there is love; And when you work with love you bind yourself to yourself, and to one another, and to God. . . . Work is love made visible.[16]

Of Joy and Sorrow he comforts:

The deeper that sorrow carves into your being, the more joy you can contain.[17]

Of Reason and Passion he says:

Your reason and your passion are the rudder and the sails of your seafaring soul.

Among the hills, when you sit in the cool shade of the white poplars, sharing the peace and serenity of distant fields and meadows—then let your heart say in silence, "God rests in reason." And when the storm comes, and the mighty wind shakes the forest, and thunder and lightning proclaim the majesty of the sky—then let your heart say in awe, "God moves in passion." And since you are a breath in God's sphere, and a leaf in God's forest, you too should rest in reason and move in passion.[18]

Of Pain he says:

Your pain is the breaking of the shell that encloses your
understanding.
Even as the stone of the fruit must break, that its heart
may stand in the sun, so must you know pain. . . .
[T]rust the physician, and drink his remedy in silence
and tranquility:

> For his hand, though heavy and hard, is guided by the
> tender hand of the Unseen,
> And the cup he brings, though it burn your lips, has been
> fashioned of the clay which the Potter has moistened
> with His own sacred tears.[19]

About God he says:

> And if you would know God, be not therefore a solver of riddles.
> Rather look about you and you shall see Him playing with
> your children.
> And look into space; you shall see Him walking in the cloud,
> outstretching His arms in the lightning and descending in rain. You
> shall see Him smiling in flowers, then rising and waving His hands
> in trees.[20]

On Death he writes:

> For life and death are one, even as the river and the sea are one.
> . . . And what is to cease breathing, but to free the breath from
> its restless tides, that it may rise and expand and seek God unen-
> cumbered? Only when you drink from the river of silence shall
> you indeed sing. And when you have reached the mountain top,
> then you shall begin to climb. And when the earth shall claim
> your limbs, then shall you truly dance.[21]

Kahlil's thoughts on death are complemented by a powerful drawing of a soul in human form, depicted in varying stages of arising as
if stretching up toward heaven and at last awakening. What struck
'me when I first saw Kahlil's painting for his section on "death" was
that I would not have labeled it as such. Its images instead reminded
me of Michelangelo's celebrated fresco on the Sistine Chapel ceiling titled *The Creation of Adam.* Kahlil's artistic interpretation is full
of movement. It is active and engaging, not a life disappearing into
the unknown ether of the afterlife but rather a life finding a long-
sought-after wholeness and being gathered into the folds of eternity.

I recall visiting Rome once during Holy Week. It was not my
first visit to the Vatican, but this time, having the opportunity to

introduce my family to these great works of art made it all the more memorable. After winding our way through vast marble halls of countless masterpieces, we finally entered the magnificent Sistine Chapel in which *The Creation* awaited. A sea of other pilgrims filled the room, and a uniformed docent called in a strained loud whisper, "silence," "*silenzio*," over and over. Perceiving the atmosphere as raucous, he made it extremely clear that we were to enter this awe-inspiring chapel with a sense of reverence. The respect was definitely present, but it was being communicated with unabashed words of wonder in a chorus of different languages, necks strained upward in admiration. Just as so many over the last five hundred years have felt a divine spark of inspiration in Michelangelo's masterpiece, I felt it as I reflected on Kahlil's work on "death."

At the Toronto International Film Festival (TIFF), I had the privilege of attending the premiere of the animated adaptation of *The Prophet*, a feature film inspired and produced by actor Salma Hayek and written and directed by Roger Allers, best known for *The Lion King*. The film was a visual extravaganza, with animated "chapters" from award-winning animation directors from around the world and beautiful music featuring world-class musicians, singers, and composers, such as Yo-Yo Ma and Gabriel Yared. It was a deeply moving experience. In fact, it was the only time, with the exception of the film *Gandhi*, that I have observed such reverent silence in a cinema when the film ended. No one in the diverse audience from all over the world moved or said a thing.

Later, at the after-party, I had the opportunity of talking with Salma about her inspiration in producing the film, which had been quite a challenge. With her contagious exuberance, she enthusiastically shared with us why she was so passionate about making the film.

My grandfather, whom I adored, was Lebanese, and he had *The Prophet* on his bedside table. We were very close and he died when I was six. He was the first person that was close to me that died. I really wished he had stayed with me, you know, to teach me about life. When I was about eighteen years old I found the book again. I recognized the cover from the book on his bedside table. I read it and when I read this book I felt it was my grandfather coming to me, to teach me about life, and about who he was. So through this book I found my grandfather again. It really felt like he was talking to me through the words of Kahlil Gibran. So this book represents a very personal experience for me. Then I found out that there are millions of people around the world who have shared the same kind of connection to this book . . . in which the words of Kahlil have so strongly impacted them positively and spiritually. So I thought that it would be important that future generations don't ever forget about him.

And especially at this time, I thought it was crucial that we pay further tribute to this man who was an Arab who wrote a book of spiritual philosophy that unites all religions and all countries and all creeds, from many different generations . . . because it talks about the simple things of life . . . that bring us all together. When you read this book, something really strange happens . . . you read something and you go, "I recognize that." And not because your brain goes back to a file that says I heard it before here or there, but because your soul recognizes it as the truth. This is why it speaks to people from all religions. This is where the dream began to turn *The Prophet* into a movie. And I wanted to make the film into an experience that people who see it have . . . all human beings from three to 103 years of age. And we thought that animation was the right vehicle to do it, to make the book come to life, because art is limitless. We could take the poetry and turn it into beautiful artworks. The film takes you on many journeys, but each time the destination is the same . . . the journey is inside of you, which is what Kahlil was all about.

Salma very clearly expressed the profound magnetism of *The Prophet* and its transformational influence on people's lives. It is a work that truly mutes religious distinctions. Finding a way to powerfully communicate a nonsectarian version of spirituality was something that weighed heavily on Kahlil. He felt a sense of sacred responsibility in writing *The Prophet*, almost as if it was to be a holy book. Even the process of writing it was a type of spiritual rebirth for him. He felt that all the events of his life seemed to lead to the writing of this book.

> It is the biggest challenge in my life. My entire being is in *The Prophet*. Everything I have ever done before . . . was only a prelude to this.[22]

In anticipation of a planned visit by Mary in the spring of 1918, Kahlil wrote of his plans for *The Prophet*.

> One *large thought* is filling my mind and my heart; and I want so much to give it form before you and I meet.[23]

During their visit, Mary records in her journal a discussion concerning the emerging manuscript. She had asked Kahlil if he would address a separate section about God in the book and he responded:

> Of Him I have been speaking in everything. I am not trying to write poetry. I am trying to express thoughts. I want the rhythm and the words right so that they shan't be noticed but shall just sink in like water into cloth.[24]

One of Kahlil's biographers, Alexandre Najjar, writes of Kahlil and *The Prophet*:

> With poetry, Gibran delivers a spiritual message inviting the reader to the fulfillment of the self and a deeper thirst for life. . . . Gibran was able to condense wisdom of all religions in a work with a universal message. It belongs to no school. . . . For him, the only doctrine that was worth defending was the doctrine of life itself.

> One day he said to [his assistant] Barbara Young, "I am a life-ist."
> Bard of life—as "life is hope itself"—the author of *The Prophet*
> chanted life till the very end.[25]

In early 1922 Mary developed a relationship with Jacob Florence
Minis, a wealthy Georgian landowner and widower of her older
cousin. Significantly older than Mary, he had grown lonely after his
wife's death and asked her to come live with him as his companion
and hostess. It would mean giving up her teaching life, and the decision caused her considerable angst. After much debate she agreed
to the arrangement and moved to live in Savannah, ultimately marrying him.

Kahlil sent a copy of *The Prophet* to Mary in Georgia upon its
publication. She wrote to him in response:

> *The Prophet* came today, and it did more than realize my hopes.
> For it seemed in its compacted form to open further new doors
> of desire and imagination in me, and to create about itself
> the universe in nimbus, so that I read it as at the center of all
> things. The format is excellent and lets the ideas and the verse
> flow quite unhampered. The pictures make my heart jump
> when I see them. They are beautifully done. . . . And the text
> is more beautiful, nearer, more revealing, more marvelous in
> conveying Reality . . . than ever. . . . The English, the style,
> the wording, the music—is exquisite, Kahlil—just sheerly
> beautiful. . . . This book will be held as one of the treasures
> of English literature. And in our darkness we will open it to
> find ourselves again and the heaven and earth within ourselves.
> Generations will not exhaust it, but instead, generation after
> generation will find in the book what they would fain be—and
> it will be better loved as men grow riper and riper. It is the
> most loving book ever written.[26]

I visited the charming coastal Georgian city of Savannah when the
magnolia trees were in full bloom. Staying at the historic Marshall
House, I enjoyed taking in the many manicured squares, stately
manors, antebellum architecture, and cobblestoned streets lined

with oak trees covered in Spanish moss. It was not difficult to imagine Mary moving to this charming city after her many years in New York. I had written ahead to arrange a meeting with Tania Sammons, a curator at the Telfair Museum of Art, where much of Kahlil's art is preserved. Due to Mary's close association with Savannah and the Telfair Museum, she chose to bequeath her treasured collection of Kahlil's work—102 drawings, watercolors, paintings, and pastels—into their care. While she also donated her correspondence with Kahlil to the University of North Carolina and a few drawings and paintings to the Metropolitan Museum of Art, the Newark Museum, and the Boston Museum of Fine Arts, the majority of her collection was given to the Telfair.

Tania, a specialist on Gibran, hosted me generously and accompanied me to the back archives to show me Kahlil's art in their collection. The majority were drawings, but there were a few paintings as well. The drawings were not framed but carefully preserved in individual folders. As I looked through each work, taking notes, Tania shared how she was in the process of writing a biography on Mary Haskell and told me how to find her former home afterward. After a scenic walk of twenty blocks, I spent some time in front of Mary's former house; full of Southern allure, a modest albeit stately home, it is a normal residence now and sits on the corner of beautiful Forsyth Park. I then walked over and sat down on the park bench made famous in the movie *Forrest Gump*, imagining Mary writing Kahlil from Savannah, reading and editing his work, and reflecting on the artwork he sent her.

While in Savannah I spoke by telephone to one of Kahlil's biographers, Suheil Bushrui, a professor at the University of Maryland, about the unique influence and spirituality of Kahlil. Dr. Bushrui took great care to highlight to me that Kahlil did not accept the schism between the divine and material aspects of civilization. He emphasized that Kahlil had been influenced by Ibn al Arabi, the thirteenth-century Sufi mystic, who saw only the oneness of humanity.

> In *The Prophet*, Gibran is simplifying Islam and Christianity . . . to the essence of what they are about. His Almustapha, in *The Prophet*, was bringing Jesus and Mohammed together.[27]

Through the voice of his literary mystical prophet, Almustafa, Kahlil seems to have found a way in which to merge admired aspects of the Sufi Muslim tradition with the Christian mystical heritage of his own Maronite Christian background. Influenced by the mysticism in Islam, it is worth noting the beautiful verse in the Qur'an that speaks so visually of this nearness.

> *We* created man. *We* knew the promptings of his soul, and are closer to him than his jugular vein. (50:16)

Barbara Young said of Kahlil:

> Gibran found himself outside the religious faith to which he had been born. And he found no other organized and formulated "religion" that he could embrace.[28]

Of Kahlil's belief in God, one of his biographers, Alexandre Najjar, writes:

> What kind of God did Gibran believe in? His view of God was not mainstream. Gibran's mysticism is a convergence of several different influences: Christianity, Islam, Sufism, theosophy and Jungian psychology. . . . He was a native of Lebanon, which, contrary to appearances, represented religious syncretism, a message of coexistence. . . . He rejected fanaticism and religious segregation of any kind and culled his own convictions from a synthesis of different religious messages without their dogmatism. He . . . could not reasonably confine himself to any one of the three great monotheistic religions.[29]

Najjar also comments specifically on Kahlil's book *The Prophet*:

Gibran brings everything back to God. . . . Gibran calls for aspiration to a "Giant Self" by opening our hearts to love and invites us to a mystical flight towards the perfect world. . . . *The Prophet* is a book that abounds in hope and optimism.[30]

There is a sense in which God is so intimately a part of our every breath, and at the same time so large as to fill the Universe. Kahlil felt that to search for God solely in a mosque, a church, or a temple is to limit one's search for wholeness. Almost a decade earlier in Kahlil's collection of parables and poems, *A Tear and a Smile*, he conveyed his belief in unity across religious divides:

> You are my brother and I love you.
> I love you when you prostrate yourself in your mosque,
>   and kneel in your church, and pray in your synagogue.
> You and I are sons of one faith—the Spirit.[31]

In Kahlil's essay "Open Letter from a Christian Poet to Muslims," just before the onset of the First World War, he referred to himself as a Christian who placed "Jesus in one half of his heart and Mohammed in the other."[32] When I visited the Gibran Museum in Lebanon, I saw on display several books on Muhammad that Kahlil owned. One in particular was a popular book written by David Samuel Margoliouth, an Orientalist, Oxford professor of Arabic, and priest in the Church of England, during Kahlil's lifetime. Next to it was a copy of Kahlil's Bible.

When Kahlil was befriended by Ameen Rihani in Paris as a young man, Rihani was already writing of the unity of all religions, which no doubt impacted Kahlil during a formative stage of his life. In his poem "A Chant of Mystics," Rihani wrote:

> Nor Crescent nor Cross we adore;
> Nor Buddha nor Christ we implore;
> Nor Muslim nor Jew we abhor;
> We are free . . .
> We are not of the East or the West;
> No boundaries exist in our breast:
> We are free.[33]

Kahlil expressed this same universal spiritual embrace in his work titled "Your Thought and Mine," often seen as his "creed," which includes these words,

> You have your thought and I have mine.
> Your thought advocates Judaism, Brahmanism, Buddhism, Christianity, and Islam.
> In my thought there is only one universal religion, whose varied paths are but the fingers of the loving hand of the Supreme Being.
> You have your thought and I have mine.[34]

On their return voyage to America after Kahlil's two years in Paris, he and Rihani stopped in London to explore the art of the city. Kahlil especially resonated with the art of William Turner at the Tate Gallery, now known as the Tate Britain, and of course of the mystic poet-painter William Blake. Their friend Yusif Huwayyik, whom Kahlil had known since high school days in Beirut, was touring with them as well. Yusif's uncle was a Maronite patriarch and his grandfather had been a priest in Bsharri. While there, the three compatriots, all from Maronite Christian backgrounds, came up with an ambitious plan to inspire reconciliation between faiths in the Arab world on a grand artistic scale. Pivotal to their plans was the construction of an opera house in Beirut showcasing two domes, one resembling a church basilica and the other featuring mosque minarets, symbolizing the reconciliation of Christianity and Islam. Although the plans never materialized, the desire was there.[35]

Following his writing of *The Prophet*, Kahlil put together a book of aphorisms in English called *Sand and Foam*, and his own decorative designs enhanced its pages. As if emerging from a vast ocean of sand and foam, they offer insightful grains of wisdom, both illuminating and inspiring, that echoed the universal spirituality of *The Prophet*. He wrote:

> Should you really open your eyes and see, you would
>   behold your image in all images. And should you open
>   your ears and listen, you would hear your own voice in
>   all voices.[36]
> Many a doctrine is like a window pane.
> We see truth through it but it divides us from truth.[37]

On one of my visits to the Gibran Museum in Bsharri I was able to sit down and talk with the now late curator, Wahib Kayrouz. He told me that to understand Kahlil it was necessary to consider the words he had spoken of himself:

> My life is a life interior.[38]

Such a simple statement, but so illuminating as to the essence of who Kahlil was and the depth of the Eastern and Western spiritual reservoirs from which he drew. One of Kahlil's most iconic drawings on display at the Gibran Museum is the *Face of Almustafa, the Prophet*. As in earlier books, Kahlil illustrated *The Prophet* with his own ethereal drawings throughout. He had created this depiction of Almustafa to be the frontispiece for *The Prophet*, and it is the first thing one sees when opening a first-edition copy. According to Kayrouz, it took him six years to perfect it, experimenting with both pencil and charcoal.[39] His three drawings of what he saw as a sacred face are on display in Bsharri. Familiar with Coptic icons from my years in Egypt, the face of the Prophet reminds me of the work of an icon writer. It is infused with a sense of infinite luminous revelation, a sort of eternal light shining through a veil of transparency, lingering between worlds.

Mary recorded Kahlil's comments on this drawing in her journal:

> I told you, did I not, how I saw the face of the Prophet? I was
> reading one night in bed late and I stopped, weary, and closed my

eyes for a moment. When I closed my eyes, I saw quite plainly that Face. I saw it for one or two minutes, perfectly clearly, and then it disappeared. The Prophet was my attempt to reproduce the Jesus face. And how I have worked on The Prophet![40]

Kahlil succeeded at crafting a poetic invitation to journey toward the depths of one's self. Uniquely embodying the East and West, his own spiritual search led him to move beyond the borders of creeds and cultures and into another dimension of spirituality. Insightfully exploring the motivations and aspirations of the human mind and heart, it is a work of boundless inspiration.

During a visit to Bsharri I met a woman who, while walking through the Gibran Museum, was tightly clutching her first edition, first print run copy of The Prophet, signed by Kahlil himself. It was clearly a treasured possession. She explained to me that due to the way his spirituality had transformed her life, she was now in search of a first edition copy of the book he had written after The Prophet, as it further helped her understand his spiritual depth. That next book was Jesus the Son of Man.

The Son of Man

*My art can find no better resting place than the
personality of Jesus.
His life is the symbol of Humanity.
He shall always be the supreme figure of all ages
and in Him we shall always find mystery, passion,
love, imagination, tragedy, beauty, romance and truth.*

—KAHLIL GIBRAN[1]

THE THIRTEENTH-CENTURY SUFI MYSTIC IBN AL ARABI
wrote, "The person who catches the disease of Christ
can never be cured." How true this was for Kahlil, who
caught this sweet contagion at a young age and was captivated
with the personality of Jesus throughout his life. Kahlil was inspired early on by sages. Whether in person or through the pages
of a book, he admired and was influenced by many different types
of mentors who spurred him on toward inner spiritual depth and
artistic distinction. As far back as his childhood in Lebanon, he
spoke with deep affection of Father Yusef, his village priest, and
the positive role he played in his life. He thrived on his relation-
ships with artists and mentors such as Fred Holland Day and Albert Pinkham Ryder and the opportunity to meet Auguste Rodin,

Rabindranath Tagore, and `Abdu'l-Bahá. He esteemed the work of da Vinci as a child and valued the kindred spirit he found in the life and writings of William Blake. His own created sage in *The Prophet*, Almustafa, was an accumulation of all he admired and thought wise and true. Yet he found the supreme sage in Jesus, whom he saw as *The Supreme Light*, as he titled one of his paintings. His ever-increasing fascination with Jesus was a thread woven throughout his entire life, and he searched passionately for ways to creatively present the inner Christ, whose path he sought to walk.

Kahlil consecrated his "hermitage" studio in New York as a sacred space of sorts in a way that facilitated both contemplation and inspiration. On his wall hung a large, old Armenian tapestry depicting the crucifixion of Christ surrounded by mourners and the two thieves, all portrayed with Asian features. Kahlil called the tapestry his "altar piece" and referred to Jesus's expression on it as what he sought to depict in his writings and art on Christ. I saw this striking tapestry, albeit now frayed and threadbare, when I visited the Gibran Museum in Bsharri and learned from its now late curator, Wahib Kayrouz, that it had been made by someone known as Father Yaqoub. Kahlil said of his precious tapestry:

> You can't imagine how wonderful it is to live with. It makes everything else look small. It is the only crucifixion I have ever seen in which Jesus is blessing with his right hand—and there is no blood from either hand, nor from the feet or the side.[2]

As one studies Kahlil's life, reads his writings, and admires his paintings, his fascination with Jesus's magnetic personality is compelling, even contagious. From his early years in Lebanon to his close association within the Lebanese immigrant community in America, Kahlil found himself naturally surrounded by those who deeply venerated Jesus. The Maronite Catholic Church, to which his family belonged, would have passionately advocated an allegiance of belief in Christ. Everywhere in his Christian religious community, he would have found himself face to face with images or statuary of Jesus, from icons and sculptures in front of churches to crucifixes on walls and jewelry or on the ends of prayer rosaries. However, observing the corruption and inequalities of the church in Lebanon as a young man, he was at the same time drawn to the revolutionary aspect of Jesus's all-embracing love and the strength of his humility.

As approximately an equal number of Lebanese are Muslim, he would have also found a deep respect for Jesus (known by his Qur'anic name, *Isa*) in Islam, which has had a preoccupation with Jesus spanning more than fourteen hundred years. As in the Christian tradition, Muslims also see Jesus as the origin of the Gospels (referred to as the *Injil*), believe in the virgin birth, call him the Messiah, and even believe in his eventual return. As renowned Cambridge Professor Tarif Khalidi, a Lebanese of Muslim background and the author of *The Muslim Jesus*, wrote, "[In Islam] there exists a preoccupation with Jesus that is unique among the world's non-Christian religions. . . . Islamic culture presents us with what in quantity and quality are the richest images of Jesus in any non-Christian culture. No other world religion known to me has devoted so much loving attention to both the Jesus of history and the Christ of eternity."[3]

Kahlil would naturally have been attracted to the mysticism within Islam known as Sufism. Sufis are particularly sympathetic to Christ, calling him "the prophet of the heart." Sufism is known for its flexibility and wide variety, focusing on a different concept of approaching God, with the aim being union with God. Interestingly, much of Sufism bears a Christian resemblance. During the history of Islam, Sufis such as al Hallaj, Sahra Wardi, Ibn al Arabi, Hafez, and Jalal al-Din Rumi, the great Sufi poet, have tried to interpret Islam in fresh ways. In so doing Sufis have often looked to Christ as their model of self-sacrifice for God. For example, al Hallaj, the tenth-century Sufi martyr, loved Jesus and tried to closely identify with him, choosing Jesus as his life model and even choosing, when sentenced to death in Baghdad, to be crucified like Christ.

Kahlil expressed a lifelong belief that Jesus's entrance onto the world stage was the most important event in human history and considered him the supreme figure of all ages. He was long fascinated with the person of Jesus, and his desire to write a book about him had been fermenting for more than twenty years. He chose to refer to Jesus in the way that Jesus mysteriously and most frequently referred to himself, "Son of Man." It was a somewhat ambiguous title during Christ's time, associated with a figure mentioned in the book of Daniel in the Hebrew Bible who would serve as a representative of God to the people. In referring to himself as the "Son of Man," Jesus was breaking stereotypes and creating for himself a new category, completely unencumbered by extraneous associations, as he refused to be enslaved by people's paradigms, which Kahlil clearly understood and admired.

Barbara Young wrote insightfully of Kahlil's admiration of Jesus:

> He regards Jesus as the most humanly enlightened . . . a supreme poet. . . . Gibran believes that Jesus lived his human life to the full, that there was no cup of human rapture that he did not drink, no extremity of human anguish that he did not comprehend and share in his divinity, and that withal there was no shadow, no blemish upon his life.[4] From his earliest years his passionate devotion was given to Jesus, of whom he said in his youth that He was "the most supremely good and wise of all the wise and good who have walked the Earth; Jesus, our Lord and our Brother; Jesus, the Son of Man."[5]

I have come across people all over the world, regardless of religious tradition, from Tuareg nomads in Timbuktu in the Sahara Desert to investment bankers in Hong Kong, who were inexplicably drawn to the person of Jesus. And like Kahlil, it is always the Jesus of the Gospels that attracted them, as opposed to the Christ of the Christian Church—a Jesus without all the religious or cultural associations that have accumulated around him over the past two thousand years. I have met Buddhist monks in Sri Lanka who became followers of Jesus, seeing him as their "Grand Master" within their Buddhist tradition. And Hindus in India who see Jesus as Mahatma Gandhi did, who said that Jesus "expressed, as no other could, the spirit and the will of God. . . . The lives of all have, in some greater or lesser degree, been changed by His presence, His actions, and the words spoken by His divine voice. . . . And because the life of Jesus has the significance and the transcendency to which I have alluded I believe that He belongs not solely to Christianity, but to the entire world; to all races and people."[6] The words of the great Bengali Hindu poet, philosopher, and Nobel laureate Rabindranath Tagore, Kahlil's literary contemporary whom he so deeply admired, come to mind: "Great-souled Christ . . . we who are not Christians bow before you. We love you and worship you, we non-Christians."[7] I am reminded of the life of Sadhu Sundar Singh, the renowned Indian Sikh mystic and holy man who traveled through the Himalayas into northern India and Tibet, teaching about Jesus during Kahlil's lifetime. In the Middle East I have met Muslim imams who through their personal study of the Gospels, the *Injil*, decided to become followers of Jesus and his teaching and yet remain in their roles in their mosques. I have even been introduced to a Bedouin Muslim tribe whose *shaykh*, captivated with Jesus's life and message, led them all to follow in the way of Christ's teachings.

Before assembling his thoughts on paper, Kahlil spoke to his friend Mischa about his idea to write a book on Jesus:

[W]hat do you say of a book on Jesus? Jesus has been haunting my heart and my imagination. . . . I am sick and tired, Mischa, of people who profess to believe in him, yet always speak of him and paint him as if he were but a sweet lady with a beard. . . . My Jesus is human like you and me. . . . I propose to have a number of Jesus' contemporaries speak of him, each from his own point of view. Their views combined will bring out the portrait of Jesus as I see him. The scheme will be in perfect harmony with my style.[8]

Commenting on Kahlil's approach to writing about Jesus, Mischa wrote, "[Gibran] writes of Jesus not as a historian or as a scholar, but as a poet and an artist. . . . Gibran writes of Jesus with a heart full of admiration, love and reverence; for Jesus to him had always been the very noblest and the very loftiest human ideal."[9]

Years earlier, when visiting his sister Marianna after his study period in Paris, he spoke with her about his fascination with Jesus, telling her that he had read everything he could find about Jesus.

Kahlil was especially impressed with French philosopher and historian Ernest Renan's *Life of Jesus*, which I saw in Kahlil's library at the Gibran Museum in Bsharri. Kahlil wrote of Renan:

> At the moment I am reading Renan. I like him because he loved and understood Jesus. He saw him in the light of day, not at dusk.[10]

Renan, a French expert of ancient Middle Eastern languages and civilization, was inspired to write *Life of Jesus* while on a trip to Syria and Palestine with his sister, who died suddenly of a fever she contracted. It was published in 1863 and, while controversial, was hugely popular. With only the New Testament and a copy of the first-century Jewish historian Josephus's work of history as his references, he portrayed Jesus as human, albeit in direct communion with God his Father, who did not preach dogma but instead taught us how to live. Halfway through the book, Jesus heads back to Galilee, disillusioned with the Jewish faith and spurning all religion that was not of the heart.

Another important book related to Jesus that I noticed among Kahlil's personal library was Albert Schweitzer's *The Quest of the Historical Jesus*, a groundbreaking book at the time, using the historical method to provide a portrait of the life of Christ. Like Kahlil's understanding of Jesus's importance, Schweitzer's conclusion calls his readers to follow Jesus's teachings regardless of one's theology. The German Nobel Peace Prize laureate, theologian, and renowned concert organist, Schweitzer ended up as a medical missionary in the river town of Lambaréné in French Equatorial Africa (now Gabon) as a result of his own "quest for the historical Jesus." He published a book in 1910 by that same title, which quickly became a classic. His own study of Jesus's life was so personally transformative that it led him to leave his career as a prominent theologian and musician to become a doctor and move to Central Africa to help the suffering there who had no medical care. He did this for the rest of his life. I once had the opportunity of visiting the Albert Schweitzer Hospital, which he founded on the bank of the Ogooué River, just south of the equator in lush rain forest. As I sat on a roughly hewn bench of *okoumé* wood on the riverbank, it was deeply inspiring to observe the hundreds of Bantu people being assisted by the hospital, all resulting from one man's decision to attempt to follow in Jesus's example.

I also noticed among Kahlil's books Leo Tolstoy's *The Kingdom of God Is Within You*, a philosophical treatise based on the teachings of Christ that had a profound and lasting influence on Mahatma Gandhi, who first read it as a young protester in South Africa. Gandhi wrote in his autobiography, *The Story of My Experiments with Truth*, that this book "overwhelmed" him and "left an abiding impression." Gandhi listed Tolstoy's book as one of the three most important modern influences in his life, laying the foundation for what was to become known as his nonviolent resistance movement during the years 1918 to 1947. In 1908 Tolstoy wrote a letter to Gandhi, known as "A Letter to a Hindu," which outlines the notion that only by using love as a weapon as Christ taught, through passive resistance, could the Indian people overthrow the colonial British Empire. The two continued a correspondence about the theological basis of nonviolence until Tolstoy's death in 1910. In fact, Tolstoy's last letter to Gandhi was one of his final writings, perhaps even the last.

Kahlil considered Jesus to be the greatest of all artists and poets.[11] Over the years Mary Haskell recorded pages of his dreams and thoughts about Jesus. From Paris Kahlil wrote her:

> My greatest hope now is to be able to paint the life of Jesus as no one did before. My life can find no better resting place than the personality of Jesus. . . . And [referring to a dream] I have been

all through his country from Syria to Lower Palestine. And all my life the wonder of him has grown on me.[12]

In Mischa's description of Kahlil's drawings of Jesus we find no "sweet lady with a beard."

> How does Jesus look as drawn by Gibran's pencil? A beautiful and a noble face delicately veiled with something expressive of pity gripping the heart, rather than of sorrow crouching in the soul. In the sensitive mouth is a firmness too gentle to wound, and a self-respect too proud to be meek. In the nose is the sweetness of poetry, the harmony of art and the symmetry of architecture. The eyes look through and far beyond whatever material objects they may seem to fall upon. They are inspired, but not serene; and hopeful of ultimate victory, but not yet victorious. They speak of loneliness unsoothed by Love, and of solitude uncomforted by its own light. The slightly knitted eyebrows seem to speak of a mind straining after a secret not yet revealed, or an aim not yet attained. They suggest that the man has reached the threshold of that secret whose door remains locked in his face. In his high and broad forehead is an aloof majesty. The soft hair brushed back from the brow and the temples and descending to the shoulders is eloquent of purity, immaculate and unsoiled. On the whole it is a face suggestive of many meanings, the most pronounced of them being a will that has not yet conquered, but is determined to conquer.[13]

Even in his sleep throughout the years, Kahlil often dreamed of Jesus coming to him, walking with him, sitting with him, talking to him. He pictured Jesus as a fellow Middle Easterner and felt a deep personal connection to him. The opportunity to write about Jesus's life became an ever-increasing aspiration. As a young boy in the mountains of Lebanon, his education was limited to regular visits to his village by a priest, who taught him the basics of Christian belief and the Bible and provided increased exposure to Syriac and Arabic. Syriac, the language of ancient Syria, was a western dialect of Aramaic, the language that Jesus grew up speaking. Many early Christian texts are preserved in Syriac, and it is still used by Syrian Christians as a liturgical language. Starting during his childhood, Kahlil naturally would have felt a cultural and spiritual affinity with Jesus as a Middle Eastern compatriot.

On a trip to Syria I found it profoundly moving to hear an Orthodox monk chant The Lord's Prayer in Aramaic high up in the picturesque rugged mountain village of Ma'loula, forty miles northeast of Damascus, at the fifth-century Mar Sarkis monastery, which has been partially destroyed in the Syrian civil war. Ma'loula is one of the three remaining mountain villages where Western Aramaic is still spoken. Interestingly, the local residents are both Christian and Muslim and have lived harmoniously side by side for centuries, each coming to the monastery for blessing and worship.

In March 1908 Kahlil wrote of Jesus in a letter to Mary:

> My soul is intoxicated today. For last night I dreamt of Him who gave the Kingdom of heaven to man . . . if I could only describe Him to you. . . . I sat near Him and talked to Him as if I had always lived with Him. . . . My soul is thirsty for that which is lofty and great and beautiful. And yet I cannot write nor draw nor read. I can only sit alone in silence and contemplate the Unseen.[14]

By the time Kahlil began to write his book on Jesus, he had moved beyond both the religious disillusionment of his youth and the need to antagonize religious authorities to make his point. No longer critical, he chose to soar above the fray, freely expressing himself in a creative and compelling manner. One of Kahlil's contemporary biographers commented on his intentions in his writings about Jesus:

> By plunging his Jesus deep into the turbulence of earthly existence Gibran had no wish to negate the master's divinity, but aimed instead to replace a somewhat distant conception of a figure, conjured by the church, with a more approachable personality.[15]

According to Barbara Young, on the evening of November 12, 1926, Kahlil suddenly and passionately decided to pull together all he had been mulling over in his mind and heart concerning Jesus and intensely turn his attention to the task of writing, in English, his portrayal of Jesus for the next eighteen months. A few weeks earlier he had written:

> Last night I saw his face again, clearer than I have ever seen it. It was not turned towards my face—it was looking far out into the vast night. . . . He was youth, ageless and immortal; not God, no, but the Son of Man, facing all that man must face, knowing all that man has ever known, or shall ever know. . . . He walked as a man facing into a strong wind, yet who was stronger than the wind.[16]

Despite his intent to produce a sequel to *The Prophet*, Kahlil refocused his intensity to fulfill this dream of writing about Jesus, a project that had captured his imagination and weighed heavily on his heart. Kahlil's passionate artistic portrait of Jesus was published in 1928. Titled *Jesus the Son of Man*, it received more reviews than any of his other books, and its sales were second only to *The Prophet*. John Haynes Holmes, a prominent minister and cofounder of the NAACP and the ACLU, wrote in a review for the *New York Herald Tribune*:

> Kahlil Gibran has attempted a unique and daring experiment. . . . If any man were fitted to attempt this adventurous task it is Mr. Gibran. . . . It is as though a contemporary [of Jesus] sat down at a belated hour, to write another and different Gospel.[17]

Like *The Prophet*, which foreshadowed Kahlil's creative spiritual endeavor on Jesus, he sought to further harmonize his spiritual journey through myriad voices in the search for the Son of Man. This vision culminated at a time when his health was gradually failing. Skeptical of doctors, Kahlil turned more intently to alcohol to self-medicate his pain, securing supplies of arak during the height of the Prohibition years in America.

Jesus the Son of Man was the longest and last book Kahlil wrote before his death, and some see it as a sort of "fifth gospel." Depicting the inherent alluring nature of Christ's humanity, Kahlil portrays the life of Jesus with the imagination of an artist and poet. Through the eyes and voices of seventy-seven individuals during the time of Christ, some historical and others purely fictional, some friends and others antagonists, Kahlil catches the reader off guard with the beauty of Jesus's character; from the mother of Judas grieving her son, to an angry widow in Galilee, to the tender tale of a shepherd, to concluding the book with his own voice, "A Man from Lebanon." Through vignettes we hear from the disciples; Mary, the mother of Jesus; Mary Magdalene; and from many others about how they saw and experienced Jesus, giving voice to Kahlil's own vision of the Son of Man.

Only Mary Magdalene makes more than one appearance in the book. She shares a deeply moving and beautifully vivid depiction of Jesus. Through these diverse voices Kahlil communicates that regardless of doubts, questions, or an individual's starting point (as Kahlil's Mary Magdalene at first dislikes Jesus), when the spiritual quest is done with an open mind and a sincere heart, one is undoubtedly left wordless, awestruck by the person of Jesus. Throughout the book it is obvious that Kahlil is enchanted with Jesus's character and enraptured by his teachings, and he seeks to pay tribute to him through exquisite prose.

Reflecting on his personal admiration for Christ, whom he referred to as the "Master Poet," Kahlil wrote, "in His voice, we heard a song unfathomable. . . . In my heart dwells Jesus of Galilee, the Man above men, the Poet who makes poets of us all, The Spirit who knocks at our door that we may wake and rise and walk out to meet truth naked and unencumbered."[18]

Through the vignettes in *Jesus the Son of Man*, Kahlil delivers a mesmerizing picture of the essence of Jesus. One of the earliest chapters shares the reflections of the often-controversial figure of Mary Magdalene. Interestingly, many of his chosen characters in the book are women, whom he describes with admiration and depth of spirit. Kahlil's Mary says:

> It was in the month of June when I saw Him for the first time. He was walking in the wheatfield. . . . The rhythm of His step was different from other men's, and the movement of His body was like naught I had seen before. Men do not pace the earth in that manner. And even now I do not know whether He walked fast or slow. . . . And I gazed at Him, and my soul quivered within me, for He was beautiful. . . . I left my house and walked towards Him. Was it my aloneness, or was it His fragrance, that drew me to Him? . . . Even now I do not know. . . . But when His dawn-eyes looked into my eyes all the stars of my night faded away.[19]

Later, Jesus speaks to her:

> Other men see a beauty in you that shall fade away sooner than their own years. But I see in you a beauty that shall not fade away, and in the autumn of your days that beauty shall not be afraid to gaze at itself in the mirror, and it shall not be offended. I alone love the unseen in you.[20]

As her musing concludes, she ponders:

> Then He stood up and looked at me even as the seasons might look down upon the field, and He smiled. And He said again: "all men love you for themselves. I love you for yourself." And then He walked away. But no other man ever walked the way He walked. Was it a breath born in my garden that moved to the east? Or was it a storm that would shake all things to their foundations? I knew not, but on that day the sunset of His eyes slew the dragon in me.[21]

The "Matthew" chapter is full of resplendent depth, bringing to life the Gospel writer's words:

> One harvest day Jesus called us and His other friends to the hills. The earth was fragrant, and like the daughter of a king at her wedding-feast, she wore all her jewels. And the sky was her

bridegroom. When we reached the heights Jesus stood still in the grove of laurels, and He said, "Rest here, quiet your mind and tune your heart, for I have much to tell you."[22]

Kahlil daringly goes on to paraphrase Jesus's "Sermon on the Mount":

> Blessed are the serene in spirit.
> Blessed are they who are not held by possessions, for they shall be free.
> Blessed are they who remember their pain, and in their pain await their joy.
> Blessed are they who hunger after truth and beauty, for their hunger shall bring bread, and their thirst cool water.
> Blessed are the kindly, for they shall be consoled by their own kindliness.
> Blessed are the pure in heart, for they shall be one with God.
> Blessed are the merciful, for mercy shall be in their portion.
> Blessed are the peacemakers, for their spirit shall dwell above the battle, and they shall turn the potter's field into a garden.
> Blessed are they who are hunted, for they shall be swift of foot and they shall be winged.
> Rejoice and be joyful, for you have found the kingdom of heaven within you.[23]

I remember my first visit to the Church of the Beatitudes in Galilee, built on the supposed site of where Jesus first spoke the words of his Sermon on the Mount. The small Byzantine-style church is set atop a lush green hill that slopes down into the Sea of Galilee. Surrounded by palm trees, the simple church is octagonal in shape, representing the eight beatitudes, or blessings, spoken by Jesus in his Sermon on the Mount, which echo the highest ideals of Jesus's teachings on mercy, love, humility, compassion, and peace.

After walking through the serene sacred space, as I headed toward the gardens I noticed a young man in jeans hanging out on a bench talking with his two friends. Casually slung over his shoulder was an Uzi submachine gun. While the country's citizens are allowed to openly carry guns, I found it deeply unsettling in this setting, of all places. A little later, looking back toward the church, I noticed a prominently displayed sign: "NO FIREARMS OR WEAPONS PERMITTED INSIDE THE CHURCH." Even more disconcerting was to read in the parking lot, before heading down the hill, that the church had actually been commissioned by the Italian dictator Benito Mussolini. One wonders how Kahlil would have reacted, knowing both his disdain for the institutional church aligning itself with political power and authority and his love of Jesus's message of nonviolence. Perhaps he would have remembered the words of Rabindranath Tagore, whose portrait he had painted, who was fond of asking, "What are you Christians doing? You have the clearest moral precepts in the Sermon on the Mount. Why do you not act up to them?"

Kahlil concludes his chapter on Matthew with a remarkably fresh interpretation of The Lord's Prayer.

> And Jesus said, "When you would pray, let your longing pronounce the words. It is in my longing now to pray thus:
> Our Father in earth and heaven, sacred is Thy name.
> Thy will be done with us, even as in space.
> Give us of Thy bread sufficient for the day.
> In Thy compassion forgive us and enlarge us to forgive one another.
> Guide us towards Thee and stretch down Thy hand to us in darkness.
> For Thine is the kingdom, and in Thee is our power and our fulfillment.[24]

His chapter "John the Son of Zebedee" serves as a powerful exploration of various interpretations and names for Jesus:

The Christ, He who was in the ancient of days, is the flame of God that dwells in the spirit of man. He is the breath of life that visits us. . . . He is the will of the Lord. He is the first Word, which would speak with our voice and live in our ear that we may heed and understand. And the Word of the Lord our God . . . was man like unto you and myself. For we could not hear the song of the bodiless wind nor see our greater self walking in the mist. . . . This is the Christ, the innermost and the height, who walks with man towards eternity.[25]

John's reflection continues:

And Jesus, the Man of Nazareth, was the host and the mouth-piece of the Christ, who walked with us in the sun and who called us His friends. In those days the hills of Galilee and her valleys heard naught but His voice. And I was a youth then, and trod in His path and pursued His footprints . . . to hear the words of the Christ from the lips of Jesus of Galilee. Now you would know why some of us call Him the Son of Man. He Himself desired to be called by that name, for He knew the hunger and the thirst of man, and He beheld man seeking after His greater self. The Son of Man was Christ the Gracious, who would be with us all. He was Jesus the Nazarene who would lead all His brothers to the Anointed One, even to the Word which was in the beginning with God.[26]

Kahlil gives voice to many other fictional characters in *Jesus the Son of Man*. From "Salome to a Woman Friend" we hear:

For there was no valley of hunger He could not bridge,
And no desert of thirst He could not cross.[27]

An imaginative and illusory character, "Cleopas of Bethroune" speaks of Jesus:

When Jesus spoke the whole world was hushed to listen. His words were not for our ears but rather for the elements of which God made this earth. . . . And still His speech slumbers within our breast like a love-song half forgotten, and sometimes it burns itself through to our memory. His speech was simple and joyous, and the sound of His voice was like cool water in a land of drought.[28]

"Rumanous, a Greek Poet," muses:

For in His voice there was the laughter of thunder and the tears of rain, and the joyous dancing of trees in the wind.[29]

"Benjamin the Scribe" says of Jesus:

He was an awakening.[30]

In his final chapter, "A Man from Lebanon," Kahlil himself addresses Jesus. They discuss Jesus's loyal and disloyal friends, and speak of things that have passed since the time he spent on earth. Kahlil refers to Jesus as Master Poet, Master Singer, King above all kings, Master of infinite compassion, Master of our lonely hours, Master Lover, Master of Light, Sky-heart, and Knight of our fairer dream. The book concludes:

> Poet, Singer, Great Heart,
> May our God bless your name,
> And the womb that held you, and the breasts that gave
>   you milk.
> And may God forgive us all.[31]

In the midst of writing, Kahlil labored over a drawing of Jesus to be the book's frontispiece. Years earlier, Kahlil confided in his sister that his "ultimate hope is to be able to paint the life of Jesus like no one has ever before been able to paint it."[32] This was something that he had long wished to be able to do. Even in Kahlil's work for *The Prophet*, his moving frontispiece of the Christlike character Almustafa is deeply resonant with traditional artistic expressions of Jesus. Later, after having completed his picture *Christ's Head*, he said that it was nearer to his heart than any other picture he had ever drawn.[33]

When visiting the Telfair Museum in Savannah, I was able to see six of Kahlil's drawings of Christ. All of them clearly bear the features of a Middle Easterner, as opposed to a Westernized Jesus; four were done in pencil and two in pen and ink. The drawing that struck me most powerfully is the most ordinary in form, the bent head of Christ with only his bare arm exposed. It is so human, almost hauntingly so, vulnerable and yet muscular. It is a visual expression of inner strength, intentionally gentle but not passive or vanquished in any way. Kahlil did not see Christ as a mild-mannered victim but understood him to be full of strength, as the Son of Man who walked amid the winds of the tempest.

Regarding Jesus's strength, one Good Friday he wrote in Arabic:

> Today. . . man is startled from his deep slumber and stands before the phantoms of the Ages, looking with tearful eyes . . . to witness Jesus the Nazarene nailed on the Cross. . . . For centuries Humanity has been worshipping weakness in the person of the Savior. The Nazarene was not weak! He was strong and is strong! But the people refuse to heed the true meaning of his strength.[34]

Barbara Young conveyed the response of an eight-year-old boy to the sight of one of Kahlil's portraits of Jesus: "Oh, Daddy; that is the way He looked! Why didn't the other people ever make the picture right before?"[35] And when shown to a teenager: "Well . . . I'm not religious—and I don't want to be. But I could go for a Jesus like that one."[36]

One of Kahlil's goals in writing about Jesus was to restore his identity as a Middle Easterner, which he expressed intuitively in his drawings of Christ. Not only did Kahlil's drawings of Christ highlight his Middle Eastern origin, but the settings in which he placed his characters in *Jesus the Son of Man* also bring these images to life. In early 1914 Mary recorded one of Kahlil's dreams in which he met Jesus along a road and they talked together. With detailed description he tells Mary of his appearance as a typical Middle Easterner.

> I saw Jesus coming towards me down the road. The walnuts and weeping willows arched over the road, and I could see the paths

of sunlight falling through on his face. It was the same face as always—an Arabic type of face, aquiline nose, black eyes, deepest and large, yet not weak as large eyes are so apt to be, but as masculine as anything could be, with his straight black brows. His skin was brown and healthy . . . with a thin beard like the Arabs—and his hair was abundant and black but not well kept, head bare, as always. He had on the same brown robe, loose, with a cord round the waist, and little torn at the bottom—and the same rough, heavy, common kind of large sandal on his feet—they were as usual a little dusty.[37]

In America Kahlil was undoubtedly presented a European-looking Jesus, resembling an individual more of Scandinavian roots than Middle Eastern. Due to Christianity's center of gravity moving to the West over the centuries, the portrayal of Jesus increasingly took on a European look. This Europeanization of Jesus was so successful that, ironically, even Muslim Arabs from the Middle East today often understand Jesus to be Western, when he actually came from their own culture. And of course many Westerners today perceive Christ as just like themselves, with little connection to the Middle East. As a Middle Easterner living in the West, Kahlil sought to reintroduce Jesus as the full-blooded Middle Easterner he was. Through his art and writings, he emphasized to those living in the West how critical it is to recognize and embrace Jesus's Middle Eastern origin and nature in order to most fully understand his teachings. When reading Kahlil's writings on Jesus, we are challenged to strip Jesus of his Western trappings and return him to his cultural origins, seeing him afresh as one who was born, lived, and died in the Middle East—a Jesus who first walked the Middle Eastern road.

Furthermore, Kahlil felt that this vision of Jesus as one who comes to us from the Middle East also contradicted the image of Jesus and the message of his life that was often portrayed and taught by the Church. He felt that religion, such as the institution, laws, and rituals of the Church, can even inoculate against the real Jesus. In *Sand and Foam* Kahlil shared his interpretation of Jesus:

Long ago there lived a Man who was crucified for being too loving and too lovable.

And strange to relate I met him thrice yesterday. The first time He was asking a policeman not to take a prostitute to prison; the second time He was drinking wine with an outcast; and the third time He was having a fist-fight with a promoter inside a church.[38]

In 1920 Mary Haskell recorded words Kahlil had shared with her concerning this incongruity:

> Christianity has been very far from the teaching of Christ. In the second or third century, people were not vigorous enough to take the strong food that Christ gave. . . . They could not face the gigantic self that Christ taught. . . . The greatest teaching of Christ was the Kingdom of Heaven, and that is within you. . . . But if the Kingdom of Heaven is within you, if you have that calm in yourself, that quiet in your centre, if you are in love with life, you love your enemy because you love everybody.[39]

During my conversation with Kayrouz in Bsharri at the Gibran Museum, as he showed me the handwritten drafts of *Jesus the Son of Man* that are preserved there, he highlighted the fact that the Jesus Kahlil focused on was what he liked to refer to as "Jesus of Nazareth" and Jesus's movement known as "The Way" (i.e., following in the way of Jesus), before Christianity received the official sanction of the Roman Empire and drifted further away from its Middle Eastern roots. He reiterated that Kahlil did not believe that Jesus intended to usher in a new religion, but rather to point humanity toward God and God's desired way for us to live, and to illuminate that path, walking among us as the Son of Man.

Reflecting on Kahlil's fervent attraction to Jesus, I realized how he sought to emulate the words of counsel shared with me by another writer I admired, the late Malcolm Muggeridge. As we were talking about the many interpretations of Jesus, I asked him how he believed one can discover the real Jesus. And he simply replied, "Read the Gospels and follow Jesus's teachings." Muggeridge's journey with Jesus also mirrored Kahlil's experience, when he later said, "Jesus, for me, has been a long process of discovery—a process that is by no means over, and never can be. Like an infinitely precious and rewarding human relationship which goes on developing and constantly reveals new depths and possibilities of intimacy." These are words that Kahlil would have embraced himself.

In Beirut I visited with Alexandre Najjar, a prominent lawyer and one of Lebanon's award-winning novelists. He also wrote an excellent biography on Kahlil, his countryman, and is considered an authority on him. He very generously gave me a small bust of Kahlil for my office, a miniature of the large stone sculpture outside the Gibran Museum. A practicing Maronite Catholic, Najjar has given a lot of thought to Kahlil's views of Jesus and the Church that developed around his name in the subsequent centuries.

> Gibran admits that Jesus is immortal. But it is not because he is God that he is immortal. It is because he knew how to follow the path that leads to the divine. Mankind has achieved, with and through Jesus, the perfect divine manifestation. . . . Gibran strays from the dogmas of the Catholic Church . . . and de-emphasizes the redemption. But for all that, his thesis is not so radical: well versed in the Bible, Gibran has a high opinion of Jesus and wrote texts about Him with such beauty that it is difficult to think of him as a heretic.[40]

Years earlier Kahlil shared his views on Christ and the "new path" that he sought to communicate in his *Jesus the Son of Man.*

> Christ's death, as well as his life, had a wonderful effect on his followers. The day will come when we shall think but just of the Flame—of the fullness of Life that burned in him. Socrates and his followers' relation was more mental, but Christ's followers felt him more than they felt any of his ideas. . . . Christ changed the human mind and . . . found a new path.[41]

Kahlil reminds us that if anything is true about Christianity, it is true because of Jesus, not because of Christianity. After all, Jesus wasn't even a Christian. Perhaps nothing expresses Kahlil's views of Jesus more clearly and poignantly than a powerful short story he wrote years before *Jesus the Son of Man*, which sums up everything he was trying to communicate about him.

> Once every hundred years Jesus of Nazareth meets Jesus of the Christian in a garden among the hills of Lebanon. And they talk long; and each time Jesus of Nazareth goes away saying to Jesus of the Christian, "My friend, I fear we shall never, never agree."[42]

A. Self-portrait

Kahlil Gibran (American, born Lebanon, 1883–1931), self-portrait, c. 1911; oil on Masonite, 17½ × 14½ inches. Telfair Museum of Art, Savannah, Georgia. Gift of Mary Haskell Minis, 1950.8.1.

B. Kahlil's portrait of his mother

Kahlil Gibran (American, born Lebanon, 1883–1931), portrait of the artist's mother, n.d. [Gibran's mother died in 1902]; oil on canvas, 23½ × 28¾ inches. Telfair Museum of Art, Savannah, Georgia. Gift of Mary Haskell Minis, 1950.8.43.

C. Kahlil Gibran's portrait of Auguste Rodin
Peter A. Juley & Son Collection, Smithsonian American Art Museum.

D. Mosque and dome sketch by Kahlil Gibran and Ameen Rihani for an opera house in Beirut
Two domes symbolizing the reconciliation of Christianity and Islam, signed by both; London, 1910; pencil on paper, Ameen Rihani Organization.

E. Kahlil Gibran
George William Harting (American, 1877–1943), Kahlil Gibran, April 1913; salt paper print? 11 × 6¾ inches. Telfair Museum of Art, Savannah, Georgia. Gift of Mary Haskell Minis, Telfair Museum of Art Archives.

F. Kahlil Gibran's portrait of Mary Haskell
Kahlil Gibran (American, born Lebanon, 1883–1931), Mary Haskell, 1908; charcoal on laid paper, 17¾ × 12 inches. Telfair Museum of Art, Savannah, Georgia. Gift of Mary Haskell Minis, 1950.8.71.

G. *Autumn*, a portrait by Kahlil Gibran of Micheline
l'Automne, oil on canvas; Gibran National Committee (Bsharri Museum).

H. Kahlil Gibran in his studio

Mariita (Giacobbe) Lawson, Gibran Kahlil Gibran around thirty-seven years old in his studio at 51 West 10th Street, New York, USA, August 1920; albumen print, 4¼ × 2½ inches. Telfair Museum of Art, Savannah, Georgia. Gift of Mary Haskell Minis, Telfair Museum of Art Archives.

I. Kahlil Gibran's portrait of his friend Ameen Rihani
Kahlil Gibran (American, born Lebanon, 1883–1931), Ameen Rihani, c. 1910–1915; ink on paper, 6⅝ × 5¾ inches. Telfair Museum of Art, Savannah, Georgia. Gift of Mary Haskell Minis, 1950.8.35.

J. *Almustafa* frontispiece from *The Prophet*
The face of the Prophet; charcoal, fourth stage. Gibran National Committee (Bsharri Museum).

K. Kahlil Gibran's portrait of Jesus in *Jesus the Son of Man*
Kahlil Gibran (American, born Lebanon, 1883–1931), Jesus, Son of Man; from *Jesus Son of Man: His Words and His Deeds as Told and Recorded by Those Who Knew Him*, n.d. [*Jesus, The Son of Man* was published in 1928]; graphite on paper, 47¼ × 18 inches. Telfair Museum of Art, Savannah, Georgia. Gift of Mary Haskell Minis, 1950.8.22.

L. Jesus Crucified on the Pyramid of Humanity and Religions
Jesus crucified on the pyramid of humanity and religions; charcoal, fourth stage. Gibran National Committee (Bsharri Museum).

The Wanderer   8

A traveller am I and a navigator,
and every day I discover a new region within my soul.

—KAHLIL GIBRAN, *SAND AND FOAM*[1]

GROWING UP ON THE COAST OF WEST AFRICA, not far from the Sahara Desert, I often dreamed of exotic adventures, caravanning off on a desert trek in search of parts unknown or setting off into the ocean looking for unexplored islands. One school year I sketched out rough plans to run away from my boarding school in Côte d'Ivoire and head back up along the coast to Senegal in a dugout canoe. Another year I gave one of my homing pigeons to a family friend who lived in the adjoining landlocked country of Mali. There he would release my pigeon, and I eagerly looked forward to seeing how long it would take for him to fly back home to me on Dakar's Cap-Vert Peninsula. I was to learn months later that he had set my pigeon free in the bush of Mali, only to watch him immediately fly off in the opposite direction into the Sahara Desert, never to be seen again.

Stories told in West Africa of the ancient city of Timbuktu in Mali are legendary. Renowned more as a metaphor for the "middle of nowhere," Timbuktu was a place I had always dreamed of visiting. Envisioning heavy-laden camels transporting salt blocks across shifting sand dunes, I imagined caravans in search of Timbuktu on the banks of the great Niger River. Years later, as an adult, I had the opportunity to visit the oasis town of Timbuktu numerous times and have always been fascinated by its history, surviving mud-brick buildings, ornate wooden doors, ancient mosques, old leather-bound sacred books preserved down through the centuries, and the striking flowing indigo blue robes of the Tuaregs, often known as the "Blue People." On one occasion, I was invited to the home of a Tuareg friend. To my amazement, in the midst of this remote and ancient place where caravans begin their journeys out into the vast sand sea, I noticed he had a French translation of *The Prophet* sitting prominently on his bookshelf. What a distance this book had come, still influencing hearts and minds, to the ends of the earth. Words Kahlil wrote in *The Prophet* seemed to reverberate in the barrenness of this land of nomadic wanderers.

> We wanderers, ever seeking the lonelier way, begin no day where we have ended another day; and no sunrise finds us where sunset left us. Even while the earth sleeps we travel. We are the seeds of the tenacious plant, and it is in our ripeness and our fullness of heart that we are given to the wind and are scattered.[2]

Following the publication of *The Prophet* and *Jesus the Son of Man*, life began to ease financially for Kahlil. He was able to move his sister Marianna into a more comfortable home farther out in the suburbs of Boston. Mail began to pour in with expressions of appreciation for his work. His friend Mischa remembered news of admiration from Queen Mary of Romania upon her receiving a copy of *The Prophet* from a friend. Kahlil also showed him a letter from the president of Colorado College asking permission to inscribe the words of Almustafa in *The Prophet* onto their largest chapel bell: "Yesterday is but Today's memory, and Tomorrow is Today's dream."[3]

Over the course of several years Kahlil's health slowly deteriorated, and he began to long for the land of his birth. However, he continued to push himself to work and put his affairs in order. In March 1930 he completed the final copy of his will, providing financially for his sister Marianna, giving Mary Haskell the bulk of his art and manuscripts, and requesting that his final resting place be in Bsharri. By that Christmas he was in so much pain he chose not to visit Marianna in Boston, wanting to spare her the anxiety of seeing him in that state and using work as an excuse. He was confined that month to his studio "hermitage" and only admitted his agony to May Ziadah in Cairo.

> My health at present is worse than it was at the beginning of the summer. . . . I am, May, a small volcano whose opening has been closed. If I were able today to write something great and beautiful, I would be completely cured. If I could cry out, I would gain back my health.[4]

Years earlier in a letter to Mischa, Kahlil had written of his dreams of returning to Lebanon one day.

> Since long ago I have been dreaming of a hermitage, a small garden, and a spring of water. Do you recall Yusif El Fakhri [the hermit from "The Tempest"] . . . [T]he future shall find us in a hermitage on the edge of one of the Lebanon gorges.[5]

Constantly pushing himself to work, Kahlil was able to see his book *The Earth Gods* published just weeks before his death in 1931. During a visit from Mischa, Kahlil handed him the manuscript of *The Earth Gods* and asked him to read it aloud. After discussing it, Kahlil showed him the twelve drawings he had created for the book. Mischa later noted:

> The drawings made me almost forget Gibran, myself and the poem whose music still vibrated in my ears. In addition to their lightness of touch, their depth of meaning and their harmony of lines and colors those drawings surprised me with a masculinity, a vigor, a depth and an ease never before so abundant in Gibran's art.[6]

The Earth Gods is a mythological dialogue between three gods, reminiscent of Keats's poem *Hyperion*. Some beautifully poetic passages pour forth, reflecting Kahlil's thoughts soon before he died.

> *SECOND GOD:*
> The sacred loom is given you,
> And the art to weave the fabric.
> The loom and the art shall be yours forevermore,
> And yours the dark thread and the light,
> And yours the purple and the gold.
> Yet you would grudge yourself a raiment.
> Your hands have spun man's soul
> From living air and fire,
> Yet now you would break the thread,
> And lend your versed fingers to an idle eternity.[7]

In addition to *The Earth Gods*, Kahlil was also at work on *The Garden of the Prophet*, the second book in his planned trilogy. However, rather than publishing it in the state he had left it upon his death, Barbara Young arranged it into book form, calling into question its authenticity, although his voice certainly echoes forth amid its pages.

> When darkness is upon you, say: "This darkness is dawn not yet born; and though night's travail be full upon me, yet shall dawn be born unto me even as unto the hills." . . . [W]e are the breath and fragrance of God. . . for God will not suffer Himself to be hidden from man, nor His word to lie covered in the abyss of the heart of man.[8]

The Garden of the Prophet was intended to address humanity's relationship to nature, as *The Prophet*'s focus had been on humanity's relationship with one another. The final book in the series was to explore humanity's relationship to God, a passion already infused in his life's work. Yet throughout his writings he continued to almost seamlessly weave together his thoughts on man, God, and nature, seeing them as completely intertwined. This is reflected in *The Garden of the Prophet*:

> All that is deathless in you is free unto the day and the night and cannot be housed nor fettered, for this is the will of the Most

High. You are His breath even as the wind that shall be neither caught nor caged. And I also am the breath of His breath.[9]

And what are the seasons of the years save your own thoughts changing? Spring is an awakening in your breast, and summer but a recognition of your own fruitfulness. Is not autumn the ancient in you singing a lullaby to that which is still a child in your being?

And what, I ask you, is winter save sleep big with the dreams of all the other seasons.[10]

One other fascinating piece of work Kahlil had finished but not yet published before his death was a play called *Lazarus and His Beloved*. It is a musing on death, seen from the prospective of Lazarus, who was not very happy to have been raised from the dead.

LAZARUS:

Pity, pity that I should be torn away. . . . The awakening is there where I was with my beloved and the reality. . . . my twin heart whom I sought here and did not find. . . . Then death, the angel with winged feet, came and led my longing to her longing, and I lived with her in the very heart of God. . . . We were in peace, my beloved and I . . . and it was forever the first day.[11]

The Wanderer was Kahlil's final work as his life's journey drew to a close. He completed its manuscript shortly before his death. It is a compilation of parables and sayings, ranging from the humorous to the sublime, and an expression of the unending spiritual pilgrimage in which Kahlil was engaged. The title is indeed apropos. He had earnestly wandered the road of life in search of the transcendent and allowed his unquenchable spiritual thirst to lead him to depths and new discoveries within, which he continuously sought to express. To him, the exploration and discovery were not enough; they had to be communicated and shared. In a playful revisiting of his lifelong desire for inclusivity, he wrote in one of his parables, titled "The Lightning Flash":

There was a Christian bishop in his cathedral on a stormy day, and an un-Christian woman came and stood before him, and she said, "I am not a Christian. Is there salvation for me from hellfire?" And the bishop looked upon the woman, and he answered

her saying, "Nay, there is salvation for those only who are bap-
tized of water and of the spirit." And even as he spoke a bolt from
the sky fell with thunder upon the cathedral and it was filled with
fire. And the men of the city came running, and they saved the
woman, but the bishop was consumed, food of the fire.[12]

Another short parable, "The Quest," conveys the importance
of journeying together. The story presents the dilemma of two
philosophers who are arguing over the superiority of their own
pursuit—one for the fountain of youth, the other the mystery of
death, both accusing each other of spiritual blindness. Along comes
a village simpleton and points out that they are both in search of
the same thing.

> The two philosophers looked at each other in silence for a mo-
> ment, and then they laughed also. And one of them said, "Well
> now, shall we not walk and seek together?"[13]

I remember an enjoyable afternoon I spent in California one summer wandering through the many art galleries of the picturesque
village of Carmel-by-the-Sea. This unique artist colony has long
been a haven for artists, writers, and intellectuals. Nearly one hundred art galleries can be found within one square mile. After hours
of meandering, admiring the work of well-known and local artists
alike, I came upon a small sign in the back of a gallery. Etched
into the wooden plaque were words from J. R. R. Tolkien that
made me think of Kahlil:

> Not all those who wander are lost.

Kahlil was indeed a wanderer. Yet his journey was full of intention and active seeking within and without; his was a life lived
in exploring the depths. Words that I resonate with, written by
writer Amin Maalouf in his epic novel *Leo Africanus*, reflect a
journeying identity.

> I am not from Africa, nor from Europe, nor from Arabia . . . but
> I come from no country, from no city, no tribe. I am the son of

the road, my country is the caravan, my life the most unexpected of voyages.[14]

An admirer of the Sufi poets and their manner of viewing God, the world, and the spiritual journey, Kahlil would have resonated with these words inscribed on Rumi's shrine in Konya, Turkey:

> Come, come, whoever you are
> Wanderer, worshiper, lover or leaving.
> It doesn't matter.
> Ours is not a caravan of despair.
> Come, even if you have broken your vows a thousand
>   times.
> Come, yet again, come, come.

Growing up internationally and traversing the edges of cultural identities myself, I have always been drawn to the concept of pilgrimage, seeing life as a caravan of spiritual discovery. As a teenager I loved the expressive rhythms of the Senegalese griots singing melodiously, often late into the night. I remember the electric energy of a visit from Bob Marley, his reggae music filling Dakar's stadium and spilling out into the neighborhoods nearby. I listened to the whole concert through my bedroom window. Over the years I have admired the spiritual journey of Baaba Maal, one of Senegal's internationally renowned singers. Baaba Maal is a Fulani, one of the traditionally Muslim nomadic groups in West Africa, and a member of one of Senegal's Sufi brotherhoods. His album titled *The Traveller* embodies the journeying spirit of Kahlil himself. It opens with a song titled "Fulani Rock," a high-energy, *djembe*-driven tribute to his homeland, and a stately mantra featuring a Christian choir from a church in Dakar. I love the way Baaba looks at this concept of being a traveler, both literally and metaphorically. He says:

> When you travel you learn things that would have taken you years to learn in one place. You learn about the different corners of life. . . . Most of the problems we have are because people

don't travel enough and discover other people. . . . By travelling you discover that humanity is so beautiful: different faces, different cultures, different colours, different sounds. . . . When you travel you realize that humanity and the planet is a very big gift, in spite of some of the man-made horrors. This is what I want to celebrate.[15]

Baaba Maal's music evokes the pleasures of voyaging and the satisfactions of homecoming. He explains, "No matter how long I might be away, wherever I am, and whatever I am doing, I will always return [home] to feed my soul." As Kahlil's health began to fail, his nostalgic longing for the hills of Lebanon intensified, as did his reflections on the greater meaning of life and what lay beyond: the infinite, the eternal. He truly lived his life in the world of the spirit and expressed his sense of wonder with the divine mystery at the heart of it:

If there were only one star in the firmament, one flower forever in white bloom, and one tree arising from the plain; and if the snow should fall but once in every hundred years, then we would know the generosity of the infinite.[16]

Barbara Young reflected:

His life, in terms of time, was a short life. But he neither lived nor thought in terms of time. A word constantly upon his lips was this: "We have eternity." It was a word not idly spoken. It was his creed, and it directed his life.[17]

Years earlier Kahlil wrote:

I long for Eternity, for there I shall meet my unwritten poems and my unpainted pictures.[18]

Kahlil practiced a Good Friday ritual during Holy Week for much of his life, setting it aside as a day of reflection, including the Good Friday just before his death. Barbara remembered:

It was the poet's custom to spend that day alone, in complete solitude. Then, when twilight drew on and the hour of acute remembrance of the Crucifixion had passed, he would call on the

phone and say, "Once more . . . it is finished." This he did on
that last Good Friday, just a week before he died.[19]

The Thursday after Easter 1931, Gibran lay dying. He refused to
be taken to the hospital, and the following morning he wavered
in and out of consciousness. Barbara took him to St. Vincent's
Hospital, and his sister, cousins, Mischa, a Maronite priest, and
others hurried to see him. At age forty-eight, with cirrhosis of
the liver and tuberculosis in one lung, he slipped from this world
before the day had ended, into the realm he believed would be
an endless dawn, forever the first day.

The hospital Kahlil was taken to had received survivors of the
Titanic disaster for treatment in April 1912 and was the main hospital used for treating victims of the September 11, 2001, attack
on the World Trade Center. The Sisters of Charity founded St.
Vincent's Hospital in 1849. They took care to ask Kahlil if he was
Catholic and if he wanted a priest to administer last rites. He did
not feel the need for them, as he had grown far beyond the rituals of his own faith background. Kahlil's refusal of last rites brings
to mind another spiritual wanderer, Russian writer Leo Tolstoy,
Kahlil's contemporary, and his desire at the end of his life to run
away, literally, from the pressures that were crushing in on him.
In 1910 he boarded a train in search of refuge in a monastery, on
the condition that he did not have to attend any religious services,
but he ended up having to stop at the remote railway station Asta-
povo, where he succumbed to pneumonia.

Following Kahlil's death, his body lay at the Universal Funeral
Home on Lexington Avenue for two days, where reportedly hundreds of people came to say their good-byes. The entourage of
family and friends then transferred their grieving to Boston. Mary
received a telegram from Marianna and rushed to Boston for the
funeral service in the little Church of Our Lady of the Cedars.
Under the guidance of his sister, Kahlil's request to be buried at
the monastery in Bsharri was honored. She was able to purchase
the monastery that now houses his tomb, and royalties from his
books support the Gibran Museum in Bsharri, which is dedicated
to his life and work.

In July 1931 Kahlil's remains left Providence, Rhode Island, and sailed to Beirut. Upon his arrival in Beirut, an official governmental delegation boarded the ship and a ceremonial honor guard detail stood by. Once on shore the coffin was opened and the minister of education pinned a medal of Fine Arts on his breast, conferred posthumously by governmental decree. Then began the long march from the port to the Maronite Cathedral of St. George in Beirut. In their biography, *His Life and World*, Jean and Kahlil Gibran wrote of his final return to Lebanon.

> Walking in the procession were the Minister of the Interior and representatives of the High Commissariat, the French Admiralty and the army of [French] occupation. Following them were representatives of the consular corps, the benevolent societies of all creeds, Christians, Moslems and Jews, and thousands of school children.[20]

The archbishop then blessed his body upon its arrival at the cathedral, and that evening the first president of Lebanon, prior to independence, officiated at a reception hosted by the government. Kahlil's friend Ameen Rihani was present as well and spoke movingly of their friendship. The next day it seemed the entire country paid its respects. The Gibrans continue the narrative:

> The fifty-mile route from Beirut, along the coast, and up the steep mountain to Besharri was lined with townspeople. Twenty times the swelling cortege stopped for local ceremonies. Following the body streamed men chanting martial songs and improvising poetry, while wailing women beat their breasts. At a town near Gebail ancient Byblus ceremonies evoking ancient rites to the local goddess Astarte were enacted as young men in native dress brandished swords and dancing women scattered perfume and flowers before the hearse.[21]

Blazing a rebellious and revolutionary trail in his younger years, Kahlil's wandering journey ultimately formed him into an all-embracing spiritual contemplative. He was welcomed home to his final resting place in Bsharri, not as a shunned heretic but as a revered sage and celebrated son, surrounded once again by the cedar trees he loved.

On my first visit to Kahlil's tomb in Bsharri, I was deeply moved by the setting chosen for it. Stairs in the old monastery, literally hewn out of the rocky mountainside, spiral downward toward his final resting place in the ancient grotto. The rugged walls lining the descent reminded me of Michelangelo's sculpture *The Awakening Slave*. Although carved in marble, he intentionally created an unfinished appearance in which one can visualize the emergence of a figure no longer fully trapped in stone. Michelangelo felt he was "freeing a figure that was imprisoned in the stone." So with Kahlil, his art and his words continue to echo forth, unable to be entombed or forgotten, an eternal spirit of awakening, reverberating down through time. Outside the entrance of the museum is a towering rock sculpture of Kahlil's face that is purposely only partially carved out of the stone. It profoundly expresses this sense of Kahlil's liberated spirit continuing to be released to the world.

In an unpublished poem titled "Ready Am I to Go," Kahlil wrote:

> [B]ehold the shadows of the unknown pass beneath my
>   brows,
> And hear in my last breath the echo of infinity.
> Lo, I have reached the summit; I have outstripped the
>   cries of men,
> And I hear naught save the vast hymn of this eternity.[22]

Adjacent to his final resting place is a reconstruction of his "hermitage" studio in New York that includes his small bed and a few of his easels. A portrait of Kahlil, painted by his friend Yusif Huwayyik, is displayed between two of his tall candlesticks, and a wooden plaque is inscribed with the words he wanted written on his tomb:

> I am alive like you, and now I am by your side.
> Close your eyes, look around you, and you will see me.

Following Kahlil's death, interest in his works and person heightened. Even his physical appearance became a subject of significance as his fame spread. Mary provided a comprehensive description:

> Physically, he could appear slight and weak, liable to colds, flu and stomach upsets, or sturdy and compact. He was not tall—about five foot three or four. . . . His build was slim: when healthy, he weighed about 140 pounds, but owing to his frequent bouts of ill health he was often closer to 130 pounds. His voice was quite high-pitched, and it broke relatively late in his teens. The moustache that is constant in the photographs from 1902 onwards was complemented by a trim beard for a while in the early 1920s. By 1917 his hair was grey at the temples, and in later life he wore spectacles for reading. We should imagine him with a cigarette in his hand (he smoked heavily from his time in Paris onwards), and with a cup of thick Middle Eastern coffee by his side. His energy was often tense and nervous; he paced up and down the room while working, but took little proper exercise and generally ate sparingly. His movements were graceful. His face easily reflected his mood, changing from light to dark in an instant, and he had extraordinarily expressive eyes. . . . At work in his studio, he wore Syrian clothes, but as the years went by Western suits became more his style.[23]

I traveled to Mexico City one summer with my friend Brice to visit an extensive collection of Kahlil's art purchased by Carlos Slim, one of the wealthiest men in the world who, while Mexican, is also of Lebanese descent. My own quest for this "prophet" had now spanned three continents, and my interest in his life's journey only heightened as time passed. I have always found Mexico City to be a fascinating blend of the historic and contemporary, with beautiful Spanish architecture, cultivated parks, plazas, ornate churches, and colonial palaces all amid the chaos of people, cars, canals, markets, cafes, cantinas, colorful murals, and the energetic rhythms of the country's celebratory music.

In 1934, shortly after Kahlil's death, a Lebanese immigrant in Mexico translated *The Prophet* into Spanish, and a young Syrian

Orthodox priest, also in Mexico at the time, was the first person to complete an Arabic translation. On the fiftieth anniversary of Kahlil's death, the Lebanese community in Mexico commissioned the much-loved sculptor Ramiz Barquet to sculpt a bronze bust of the poet, which was presented to Mexico City. I went to see the sculpture, still on display in a little parklike space on the corner of what is now a busy intersection in the city's Florida suburb—a tiny oasis in the midst of the crowded intensity of that metropolis.

Kahlil's work is on permanent exhibition at the Soumaya Museum. It is one of the largest collections of his work any-where in the world, housing some three hundred works of art and more than seventy manuscripts. The museum's new building is a spectacular modern architectural structure. It also holds the world's largest private collection of Auguste Rodin's art outside France. Carlos Slim's late wife, Soumaya, for whom the museum is named, was a great admirer of Rodin's work. It seemed so fitting to find Kahlil's work preserved under the same roof as the art of Rodin, who had influenced and inspired him so powerfully during his years in Paris as a young man.

While there I met with the curator, Hector Palhares Meza, and was especially taken with the many portraits and oils by Kahlil, many of which I had not seen before in other publications. The museum had a very different feel from what I had seen on display in Bsharri, which housed the majority of his more ethereal work. I saw letters of Kahlil's in English and Arabic, original manuscripts, notebooks, sketches, drawings, oil paintings, and vintage photographs, as well as his death mask and several signed first editions of his works. The museum's presentation created a real sense of what he was like on a personal level. His sense of style was evident through some of his personal items—a beautifully carved walking cane, an Art Nouveau cigarette case, and a French beret. It was clear that he loved life and lived it to the fullest. In a wonderful letter to his sister he wistfully described the excellent quality of a bottle of arak that a friend brought him.

The bulk of the collection had been gathered and preserved by Kahlil's namesake, relative, and godson, a notable Boston sculptor named Kahlil Gibran. He also collaborated with his wife, Jean, to write a comprehensive biography of his godfather. Born in Boston in 1922, Gibran remembers visits from Kahlil, his father's cousin, who inspired his artistic abilities. After his godfather's death in 1931, young Gibran became very close to Marianna, who lived in Boston as well. Years later he became her trusted and personal assistant, and when she died in 1972, she transferred responsibility to Gibran to care for all she had preserved from Kahlil. He dedicated himself to the task of preserving Kahlil's memory and enhanced the collection greatly.

Gibran also had the honor of sculpting the commemorative bas-relief portrait plaque of Kahlil I visited in Boston's Copley Square, which the mayor, along with religious and academic leaders, dedicated in 1977. In search of an institution that would be able and willing to preserve and share the collection with the world, Gibran approached Carlos Slim, and his dream came to fruition. While in Mexico City I met with the now late Patricia Jacobs Barquet, who was sent by Mr. Slim to meet with the Gibrans in Boston to assess the viability of obtaining their collection. What she discovered in their archives and vaults was beyond anything she had envisioned. She shared with me how Carlos Slim's father had loved Kahlil's work and even personally translated some of his work into Spanish. Hence, Mr. Slim grew up with a great admiration for Kahlil. While I was visiting the Soumaya Museum, he was actually in Beirut visiting Kahlil's biographer, Alexandre Najjar, to talk further about Kahlil.

Following hours spent in the museum, I ended up at the San Angel Inn, a beautiful restaurant set amid spacious gardens and fountains surrounded by whitewashed Spanish cloisters. It was the perfect setting to reflect on my exploration of Kahlil's spiritual journey, which had taken me from Lebanon all the way to Mexico. Fittingly, while reading about the restaurant's history, I learned it had originally been a Carmelite monastery, as was the museum in which Kahlil now lies in rest in Bsharri.

Kahlil's friend Mischa was at his side when he passed away at St. Vincent's Hospital. Of the experience he wrote:

> Should I feel glad for my brother's release from the cares of the earth; or should I grieve over his life, so full of storms, so rich in thought, imagination, hope, light and shade, but now picking up its hems from the earth before having had its fill of the earth? I feel the deep and awesome mystery Life is fulfilling right before my eyes. To my mind comes the words of Almustafa to the sea: Only another winding will this stream make, only another murmur in this glade, and then shall I come to you, a boundless drop to a boundless ocean.[24]

The symbolism of streams and rivers flowing into the heart of the sea is a recurring theme in Kahlil's writings. It brings to mind his journey of spiritual wandering, of his endless pilgrimage toward life's deeper dimension. In a letter to Mary, he once wrote:

> Our thirsty spirits stand now on the bank of the Great
> River.
> We drink deeply, and we are full of gladness.[25]

His allegory in *The Wanderer* titled "The River" is one of my favorites. It is frequently read at memorial services and is reminiscent of Longfellow's poem *Hiawatha*. It is set in his beloved Qadisha Valley and visually tells the story of two lives that are separate but one.

> In the valley . . . where the mighty river flows, two little streams met and spoke to one another. One stream said, "How came you, my friend, and how was your path?" And the other answered, "My path was most encumbered. The wheel of the mill was broken, and the master farmer who used to conduct me from my channel to his plants, is dead. I struggled down oozing with

the waste of those who do naught but sit and bake their laziness in the sun. But how was your path, my brother?"

And the other stream answered and said, "Mine was a different path. I came down the hills among fragrant flowers and shy willows; men and women drank of me with silvery cups, and little children paddled their rosy feet at my edges, and there was laughter all about me, and there were sweet songs. What a pity that your path was not so happy."

At that moment the river spoke with a loud voice and said, "Come in, come in, we are going to the sea. Come in, come in, speak no more. Be with me now. We are going to the sea. Come in, come in, for in me you shall forget your wanderings, sad or gay. Come in, come in. And you and I will forget all our ways when we reach the heart of our mother the sea."[26]

Kahlil saw himself first and foremost as a pilgrim, journeying toward the Divine, never feeling he had arrived. So much of religion, like Kahlil's church background, teaches their devotees 'that they "arrive" at their destination by living a certain way or believing a specific dogma. The creedal emphasis of many religions has a sense of finality to it. However, in contrast, Kahlil was a pilgrim, someone always on the move. Pilgrims embody a spirit of openness when seeking depth on their spiritual journeys. As a wanderer, Kahlil, through his life pilgrimage, beautifully affirms the words of a poetic verse from that remarkable pilgrim Psalm or, as his Muslim friends would have called it, the *Zabur.*

Blessed are those who have set their hearts on pilgrimage. (Psalm 84)

A Man for Our Times 9

Your neighbor is your other self dwelling behind a wall.
In understanding, all walls shall fall down.

—KAHLIL GIBRAN, *JESUS THE SON OF MAN*[1]

M Y LAST VISIT UP INTO THE MOUNTAINS of Bsharri
took place in the springtime. Olive trees were just beginning to bloom, overflowing streams coursed toward
the sea, and cultivated vineyards on hillsides were showing signs
of new growth. Remembering my earlier visits and the various
seasons in which I had traveled the world "in search of a prophet,"
this trip felt like a celebration of all I had discovered. Kahlil's life,
expressed so vividly through his art and writings, was a profound
reminder of the need for beauty and imagination, to seek peace
within and throughout the world, to reach beyond ourselves
and build bridges of understanding with all peoples, regardless of
creed, culture, or ethnicity.

In the midst of the increasing chasm of discord and misunderstanding that exists between the Middle East and the West
and between their creeds and cultures, our day calls for a whole
new kind of movement—not of belief, religious unity, or cultural
uniformity but rather, quite simply, one that builds on what we

hold in common. Kahlil did this innately and authentically. He experienced the oneness of creation, moved beyond religion into the realm of embracing nonsectarian spirituality, and sought to foster a culture of peace, beautifully intertwining the East and West. His search was earnest and lifelong, an inspiration to live harmoniously with God, the earth, and one another. A unique blend of East and West, Kahlil embodied the struggle for reconciliation, and his spiritual quest is an invitation to awaken and to grow into one's "greater self." His voice is timeless, full of compassion and hope, artistry and elegance, appealing to heart and mind, faith and reason. Kahlil calls each of us to be "a candle in the dark," in the words of the late Palestinian poet Mahmoud Darwish's renowned poem "Think of Others."[2]

Kahlil was a man for our times. With a foot in every camp, he embodied the words of Rumi, the great Sufi mystic.

> I am neither Christian nor Jewish, nor Muslim
> I am not of the East, nor of the West. . . .
> I have put duality away, I have seen the two worlds as
> one;
> One I seek, One I know, One I see, One I call.[3]

As Father Samir Khalil Samir, the renowned Jesuit priest and interreligious scholar, said to me over lunch in Beirut, "Gibran went beyond religion to the core of universal spirituality." It was not a forced journey but rather one of spiritual openness and discovery, leading to greater and greater transcendent depth. To Kahlil, religion served as an attempt to connect with the divine, yet he realized that could not be found solely in creeds or dogma; his search became an opportunity to unearth what God had woven into the very fabric of creation. In an age in which issues in our environment are at the forefront, with deep respect for the earth, Kahlil's holistic worldview rings forth. He did not separate the spiritual dimension of life from the natural world, but rather saw them in harmony. Insightfully, he wrote:

> Religion began when man discerned the sun's compassion on the
> seeds which he sowed in the earth.[4]

Although Kahlil often spoke directly of God, his art and writings were infused with his deeper concern, that of living in harmony with one another and all of creation. Understanding and empathy emanated from his person, ideals so necessary in our contemporary context.

> I bid you to speak not so freely of God, who is your All, but speak rather and understand one another, neighbor unto neighbor.[5]

I love the way Kahlil expresses his collective embrace of the oneness of humanity in *Sand and Foam*:

> Should you sit upon a cloud you would not see the boundary line between one country and another, nor the boundary stone between a farm and a farm. It is a pity you cannot sit upon a cloud.[6]

Kahlil came to see himself in the "other" as if standing before a mirror.

> My friend, you and I shall remain strangers unto life,
> And unto one another, and each unto himself,
> Until the day when you shall speak and I shall listen
> Deeming your voice my own voice;
> And when I shall stand before you
> Thinking myself standing before a mirror.[7]

A prophetic voice during his own lifetime, Kahlil's words are perhaps even more timely today. To heed his wisdom would heal our world. Always highlighting the importance of the spiritual side of life, he at the same time advocated finding practical and honorable solutions to the major challenges that face our world today. In a wonderful short story called "The Critics," Kahlil explored the futility of finger pointing and the need to focus on solving problems rather than creating them. He narrates the story of a man traveling on horseback who stops at an inn for the night. During the night the traveler's horse had been stolen, and rather than receiving empathy from his fellow lodgers, he found only criticism from them of his own supposed faults and shortcomings. Astonished by their treatment, he points out the obvious—that the one who stole the horse should be the focus of their attention.[8]

Kahlil sought to build bridges and tear down walls. His compatriot Khalil Hawi, Lebanon's late-twentieth-century prophetic poetic voice, was one of the most eminent pioneers of modern Arabic poetry. Words from his poem "The Bridge" visually express the essence of Kahlil's life and message.

> Why is it that our house is split in two?
> And that the sea flows between the old and new?
> A cry, the shattering of wombs,
> The tearing apart of veils.
> How can we remain beneath a single roof?
> When there are seas between us, and walls, deserts of cold
>   ash,
> And ice?
> When are we to break out of the pit and prison?
> And when O lord, are we to be strong and build with our
>   own hands
> Our new, free house?[9]

In an essay written to Middle Easterners titled "The New Frontier," Kahlil wrote a forward-thinking challenge to the children of tomorrow, which continues to ring true with hope for today.

> But the children of tomorrow are the ones called by life, and they follow it with steady steps and heads high, they are the dawn of new frontiers, no smoke will veil their eyes and no jingle of chains will drown out their voices. . . . They are like the summits, which can see and hear each other—not like caves, which cannot hear or see. They are the seed dropped by the hand of God in the field, breaking through its pod and waving its sapling leaves before the face of the sun. It shall grow into a mighty tree, its root in the heart of the earth and its branches high in the sky.[10]

Mary Haskell, who played such an enriching role in Kahlil's pursuit to create compelling visual and literary art, recorded Kahlil's musings on living a purposeful life.

If I can open a new corner in a man's own heart to him I have not lived in vain. Life itself is the thing, not joy or pain or happiness or unhappiness . . . live *your* life. . . . I am different every day—and when I am eighty, I shall still be experimenting and changing.[11]

In his own visionary words, Kahlil spoke of life's end as enabling a new dawn.

Night is over, and we children of night must die when dawn comes leaping upon the hills; and out of our ashes a mightier love shall rise.[12]

In a tribute to Kahlil, his friend Mischa wrote:

Gibran Kahlil Gibran's was of those souls that experienced moments of utter clarity in which Truth delights to be mirrored. In that was Gibran's glory. . . . Whoever knows not Gibran's sorrows cannot know his joys. And whoever knows not his joys cannot know the power that made it possible for him to put his joys and sorrows in words that ring with melody, and in colors that stand out as living thoughts and longings, and lines that are ladders between the animal in the human heart and the God enthroned within that heart. In revealing himself to himself Gibran reveals us to ourselves. In polishing the mirror of his soul he polishes the mirrors of our souls. In the same Truth he is glorified we, too, are glorified.

For some purpose unknown to you and to me Gibran was born in Lebanon at the time he was born. And for a reason hidden from you and me Arabic was his mother tongue. It would seem that the all-seeing eye perceived our spiritual drought and sent us this rain-bearing cloud to drizzle some relief to our parching souls.[13]

By capturing our imaginations and enriching our spirits, Kahlil poetically inspires us to realize what is possible, what is precious, and how we can all play a part in shaping our world into one where beauty, understanding, and compassion are valued above all.

In a simple blessing for us all, Kahlil wrote:

May the vines in your vineyard be weighted with grapes, and your threshing floors be heaped with corn, and your jars be filled with oil, honey and wine; and may God place your hand upon the heart of Life that you may feel its pulse.[14]

Timeline of the
Life of Kahlil Gibran

1883: January 6: Birth of Gibran Khalil Gibran, Bsharri, Lebanon.

1895: Emigrated with his mother, two sisters, and half-brother to Boston, USA.

1895: Khalil started school and his name was Anglicized to Kahlil Gibran. Started to learn English.

1898: Showed promise in drawing and painting. Sent back to Lebanon to Maronite school in Beirut.

1901: Returned to Boston.

1902: Visited Lebanon as an interpreter for a touring American family. Sister Sultana died in Boston.

1903: Lost his half-brother Butros (Peter) to tuberculosis and his mother to cancer.

1904: Held first art exhibition of his drawings in Boston at Fred Holland Day's studio.

1905: Published *Music* in Arabic.

1906: Published *Nymphs of the Valley* and *Spirit Brides* in Arabic.

1908: Published *Spirits Rebellious* in Arabic. Left for Paris to study art, sponsored by Mary Haskell.

1910: Returned to Boston. Joined Arab-American writers society.

1911: Started spending time in New York City. Created the artwork for Ameen Rihani's *Book of Khalid*.

1912: Moved to New York City. Published *Broken Wings* in Arabic.

1914: Published *A Tear and a Smile* in Arabic. Held exhibition at the Montross Galleries on December 14.

1917: Art exhibition held by M. Knoedler & Co. on Fifth Avenue.

1918: Alfred A. Knopf published his first book in English, *The Madman*.

1919: Published a collection of art, *Twenty Drawings*, and *The Processions* in Arabic.

1920: Published *The Tempests* in Cairo. Second book in English, *The Forerunner*, was published. Founded a literary society in New York with other Arab writers and poets.

1923: Published *The Prophet*, his most famous book. *New and the Marvelous* published in Arabic.

1926: Published *Sand and Foam* in English.

1927: Published *Kingdom of the Imagination* in English.

1928: Published *Jesus the Son of Man* in English.

1931: Published *The Earth Gods* in English. Died April 10 in New York. Buried in Bsharri, Lebanon.

Published posthumously in English:
The Wanderer (1932), *The Garden of the Prophet* (1933), *Lazarus and His Beloved* (Play, 1933)

Works translated from Arabic and published posthumously:
Tears and Laughter (1947), *A Tear and a Smile* (1950), *The Processions* (1958), *Broken Wings* (1959)

Acknowledgments

La révélation m'est venue d'Orient.
The revelation came to me from the Middle East.

—HENRI MATISSE, 1947

I AM INDEBTED TO MANY INDIVIDUALS and institutions during the journey of writing this book.

In particular, I want to express my profound thankfulness to those who took the time to share with me their knowledge and insight regarding Kahlil Gibran:

The late *Wahib Kayrouz*, who served as the illustrious curator of the Gibran Museum in Bsharri, Lebanon, for many years.

Alexandre Najjar in Beirut, one of Lebanon's award-winning novelists and a biographer of Kahlil Gibran.

Tania Sammons, a former curator at the Telfair Museums in Savannah, Georgia, and a scholar on Kahlil Gibran's patron, Mary Haskell Minis.

The late *Suheil Bushrui*, eminent scholar of Kahlil Gibran and peacemaker, who concluded his distinguished academic career at the University of Maryland.

Fr. Samir Khalil Samir in Beirut, an Egyptian Jesuit priest, scholar of Islam, and special advisor to the Vatican on Christian-Muslim relations.

Hector Palhares Meza, curator of the Soumaya Museum in Mexico City, Mexico, which has one of the largest collections of Kahlil Gibran's art and work.

The late *Patricia Jacobs Barquet* of the Archivo Inmigrantes Notables en Mexico Siglo XX in Mexico City, Mexico, who assisted the Mexican business magnate Carlos Slim in acquiring the Kahlil Gibran collection that is in his Soumaya Museum.

I also wish to express my deepest gratitude to:

Mazhar Mallouhi, noted Syrian writer, novelist, interfaith advocate, and the subject of my previous book, who hosted me so graciously in Lebanon during my visits there.

My literary agent, *John Loudon*, for his belief in this book.

Smithsonian American Art Museum, *Telfair Museums*, and *Gibran National Committee* for permission to use the images in this book, and to *Penguin Random House* for permission to quote from Kahlil Gibran's writings that are not yet in the public domain.

My editor, *Sarah Stanton*, senior acquisitions editor at Rowman & Littlefield, with whom it is a joy to work again.

Amin Maalouf, the renowned Lebanese-born French author and novelist, for being a profound inspiration through his life, writings, and friendship. He is also the most effective East-West bridge builder I have known.

To my friends throughout the Middle East and North Africa, my heart's home, for their endless, all-embracing welcome and hospitality.

Lastly, and most importantly, to *my family*, for all their assistance in myriad ways: coordinating travel, doing research, and their continual encouragement. This book could not have been written without their collaboration.

I am of course deeply indebted to many others, both in person or through their writings, but they would number too many to list. To all of them, *"Un grand merci."*

Notes

Preface

1. Jean Gibran and Kahlil Gibran, *Kahlil Gibran: His Life and World* (1974; repr., New York: Interlink, 1998), 177.

2. Haskell to Gibran, quoted in Mary Haskell's journal, October 2, 1923, in *Beloved Prophet: The Love Letters of Kahlil Gibran and Mary Haskell and Her Private Journal*, ed. Virginia Hilu (New York: Alfred A. Knopf, 1972), 416–17.

Introduction

1. Kahlil Gibran, *Spiritual Sayings of Kahlil Gibran,* trans. Anthony R. Ferris (1962; repr., Secaucus, NJ: Citadel Press, 1976), 46.

2. Daniel Rondeau, *L'Express,* November 28, 2002, http://www.najjar org/en/khalil_Gibran_en.asp.

3. Ibid.

4. M. S. Daoudi, *The Meaning of Kahlil Gibran* (Secaucus, NJ: Citadel Press, 1982), 11–12.

5. Kahlil Gibran, "The New Frontier," in *The Treasured Writings of Kahlil Gibran,* ed. Martin L. Wolf, trans. Anthony R. Ferris (Edison, NJ: Citadel Press, 1951), 775.

6. Ron Rosenbaum, "Among the Believers," *New York Times,* September 24, 1995.

7. Alexandre Najjar, *Kahlil Gibran: A Biography* (London: Saqi, 2008), 171.

8. Claude Bragdon, commendation in Kahlil Gibran, *The Prophet,* 1st ed. (New York: Alfred A. Knopf, 1923).

Chapter 1: The Sacred Valley

1. Kahlil Gibran, "The New Frontier," in *The Treasured Writings of Kahlil Gibran,* ed. Martin L. Wolf, trans. Anthony R. Ferris (Edison, NJ: Citadel Press, 1951), 518.

2. Magda Abu-Fadil, "You Have Your Lebanon: Gibran Inspires Borderless Journey across the Ages," *Huffington Post,* December 23, 2010, http://www.huffingtonpost.com/magda-abufadil/you-have-your-lebanon-gib_b_800627.html.

3. Alexandre Najjar, *Kahlil Gibran: A Biography* (London: Saqi, 2008), 20.

4. Ibid., 15.

5. Kahlil Gibran, quoted in Mary Haskell's journal, January 14, 1922, in *Beloved Prophet: The Love Letters of Kahlil Gibran and Mary Haskell and Her Private Journal,* ed. Virginia Hilu (New York: Alfred A. Knopf, 1972), 371.

6. Kahlil Gibran to Nakhli Gibran, March 15, 1908, in *Kahlil Gibran: A Self Portrait,* ed. and trans. Anthony R. Ferris (1959; repr., New York: Carol, 1990), 27.

7. Kahlil Gibran, *The Prophet* (1923; repr., New York: Alfred A. Knopf, 1992), 25.

8. Jean Gibran and Kahlil Gibran, *Kahlil Gibran: His Life and World* (1974; repr., New York: Interlink, 1998), 11.

9. Najjar, *Kahlil Gibran,* 15.

10. Mikhail Naimy, *Kahlil Gibran: A Biography* (1934; repr., New York: Philosophical Society, 1985), 20.

11. Gibran, quoted in Mary Haskell's journal, June 30, 1915, in *Beloved Prophet,* 248.

12. Gibran and Gibran, *His Life and World,* 156.

13. Kahlil Gibran, *Nymphs of the Valley,* in *The Collected Works* (New York: Alfred A. Knopf, 2007), 721.

14. Ibid.

15. Ibid., 722.

16. Ibid.

17. Ibid.

18. Retrieved from: http://yabalas.blogspot.com/2011/03/fairuz-bring-me-flute-and-sing.html.

19. A. R. Ferris, trans. Retrieved from: http://ktapoon.wordpress.com/2010/12/29/khalil-gibran-on-music/.

Chapter 2: The Heretic

1. Kahlil Gibran, *Sand and Foam,* in *The Collected Works* (New York: Alfred A. Knopf, 2007), 198.

2. Amin Maalouf, *In the Name of Identity: Violence and the Need to Belong* (1996; repr., New York: Penguin, 2003), 1, 4.

3. Aileen Vincent-Barwood, "Gibran Remembered," *Saudi Aramco World,* March/April 1983, 4–7. Retrieved from: http://www.saudiaramco world.com/issue/198302/gibran.remembered.htm.

4. Jean Gibran and Kahlil Gibran, *Kahlil Gibran: His Life and World* (1974; repr., New York: Interlink, 1998), 76.

5. Mary Haskell's journal, September 3, 1913, in *Beloved Prophet: The Love Letters of Kahlil Gibran and Mary Haskell and Her Private Journal,* ed. Virginia Hilu (New York: Alfred A. Knopf, 1972), 148.

6. Gibran, *Spirits Rebellious,* in *Collected Works,* 648.

7. Ibid., 649.

8. Ibid., 650.

9. Ibid., 651.

10. Ibid., 654, 656.

11. Ibid., 658.

12. Ibid., 658.

13. Ibid., 660.

14. Ibid., 674.

15. Ibid., 681.

16. Kahlil Gibran, *Broken Wings,* in *Kahlil Gibran: Masterpieces* (Australia: Axiom, 2005), 311.

17. Gibran, *Spirits Rebellious,* in *Collected Works,* 688.

18. Ibid., 690.

19. Gibran and Gibran, *His Life and World,* 177.

Chapter 3: The Lover

1. Kahlil Gibran, *The Prophet* (1923; repr., New York: Alfred A. Knopf, 1992), 12.

2. Suheil Bushrui and Joe Jenkins, *Kahlil Gibran: Man and Poet: A New Biography* (1998; repr., Oxford: Oneworld, 1999), 90.

3. Vincent van Gogh to Theo van Gogh, July 1880, in *The Complete Letters of Vincent van Gogh*, vol. 1 (Greenwich, CT: New York Graphic Society, 1959), 198.

4. Vincent van Gogh to Theo van Gogh, November 23, 1881, in *The Complete Letters*, 274.

5. Barbara Young, *This Man from Lebanon: A Study of Kahlil Gibran* (New York: Alfred A. Knopf, 1945), 10.

6. Kahlil Gibran to Mary Haskell, October 2, 1908, in *Beloved Prophet: The Love Letters of Kahlil Gibran and Mary Haskell and Her Private Journal*, ed. Virginia Hilu (New York: Alfred A. Knopf, 1972), 13.

7. Gibran to Haskell, November 8, 1908, in *Beloved Prophet*, 14.

8. Gibran to Haskell, June 23, 1909, in *Beloved Prophet*, 17.

9. Mikhail Naimy, *Kahlil Gibran: A Biography* (1934; repr., New York: Philosophical Society, 1985), 87.

10. Lorenzo, "Rilke and Rodin (part II)," *The Alchemist's Pillow*, February 6, 2011, http://www.alchemistspillow.com/2011/02/rilke-and-rodin -part-ii.html.

11. Ibid.

12. Naimy, *Kahlil Gibran*, 150.

13. Kahlil Gibran, "I Believe in You," in *The Treasured Writings of Kahlil Gibran*, ed. Martin L. Wolf, trans. Anthony R. Ferris (Edison, NJ: Citadel Press, 1951), 754.

14. Alexandre Najjar, *Kahlil Gibran: A Biography* (London: Saqi, 2008), 60.

15. Kahlil Gibran, *Broken Wings*, in *Kahlil Gibran: Masterpieces* (Australia: Axiom, 2005), 328.

16. Ibid., 329.

17. Young, *This Man from Lebanon*, 9.

18. Gibran, *Broken Wings*, in *Masterpieces*, 295.

19. Ibid., 299.

20. Ibid., 302.

21. Ibid., 309.

22. Ibid., 313.

23. Ibid., 317.

24. Ibid., 318.

25. Ibid., 330.

26. Ibid., 331.

27. Ibid., 335.

28. Ibid.

29. Retrieved from: http://www.poetryfoundation.org/poems-and -poets/poems/detail/43650.

30. Kahlil Gibran, *A Tear and a Smile*, in *The Collected Works* (New York: Alfred A. Knopf, 2007), 755.

31. Ibid., 757.

32. Gibran, *The Voice of the Master*, in *Treasured Writings*, 514.

33. Gibran, *A Tear and a Smile*, in *Collected Works*, 779.

34. Gibran, *The Voice of the Master*, in *Treasured Writings*, 491.

35. Gibran, *The Prophet*, 29.

36. Kahlil Gibran, *Jesus the Son of Man* (1928; repr., New York: Alfred A. Knopf, 1995), 84.

37. Gibran, quoted in Mary Haskell's journal, May 22, 1920, in *Beloved Prophet*, 339.

38. Kahlil Gibran to May Ziadah, April 6 1921, in *Love Letters: The Love Letters of Kahlil Gibran to May Ziadah*, eds. and trans. Suheil Bushrui and Salma Haffar Al-Kuzbari (1983; repr., Oxford: Oneworld, 2008), 84.

39. Young, *This Man from Lebanon*, 38.

40. Ibid., 39.

41. Ibid., 94.

42. Ibid., 3, 4.

43. Najjar, *Kahlil Gibran*, 77.

44. Gibran to Haskell, January 6, 1916, in *Beloved Prophet*, 264.

45. Gibran, *The Prophet*, 13.

Chapter 4: The Madman

1. Kahlil Gibran, *The Voice of the Master*, in *The Treasured Writings of Kahlil Gibran*, ed. Martin L. Wolf, trans. Anthony R. Ferris (Edison, NJ: Citadel Press, 1951), 473.

2. Kahlil Gibran to Mary Haskell, February 18, 1913, in *Beloved Prophet: The Love Letters of Kahlil Gibran and Mary Haskell and Her Private Journal*, ed. Virginia Hilu (New York: Alfred A. Knopf, 1972), 117.

3. Kahlil Gibran, *A Tear and a Smile,* in *The Collected Works* (New York: Alfred A. Knopf, 2007), 779.

4. Gibran to Haskell, May 26, 1911, in *Kahlil Gibran: Man and Poet*, 117.

5. Juliet Thompson, quoted in Marzieh Gail, "Juliet Remembers Gibran as Told to Marzieh Gail," *World Order* 12, no. 4 (1978), http://bahai -library.com/gail_thompson_remembers_gibran.

6. Ibid.

7. Gibran to Haskell, April 19, 1912, in *Beloved Prophet*, 74.

8. Suheil Bushrui and Joe Jenkins, *Kahlil Gibran: Man and Poet: A New Biography* (1998; repr., Oxford: Oneworld, 1999), 125.

9. Malcolm Muggeridge, *Chronicles of Wasted Time* (Vancouver: Regent College, 2006), 303.

10. Alexandre Najjar, *Kahlil Gibran: A Biography* (London: Saqi, 2008), 13.

11. Jean Gibran and Kahlil Gibran, *Kahlil Gibran: His Life and World* (1974; repr., New York: Interlink, 1998), 261.

12. Gibran to Haskell, December 13, 1914, in *Beloved Prophet*, 212.

13. Gibran, quoted in Mary Haskell's journal, April 26, 1914, in *Beloved Prophet*, 188.

14. Barbara Young, *This Man from Lebanon: A Study of Kahlil Gibran* (New York: Alfred A. Knopf, 1945), 95.

15. Mikhail Naimy, *Kahlil Gibran: A Biography* (1934; repr., New York: Philosophical Society, 1985), 252.

16. Ibid., 251.

17. V. F. Odoevsky, *Russian Nights*, trans. Olga Koshansky-Olienikov and Ralph E. Matlaw (1965; repr., Evanston, IL: Northwestern University Press, 1997), 56.

18. Ibid., 89.

19. Alexander Gilchrist, *Life of William Blake* (London: Macmillan, 1863), chap. 35.

20. Malcolm Muggeridge, *The Third Testament* (New York: Plough, 2011), 32, 42, 47.

21. Gibran, *The Madman*, in *The Collected Works*, 5.

22. Ibid., 6.

23. Ibid., 17.

24. Ibid., 31.

25. Ibid., 43.

Chapter 5: The Tempest

1. Kahlil Gibran, *Jesus the Son of Man* (1928; repr., New York: Alfred A. Knopf, 1995), 73.

2. Kahlil Gibran, *The Madman*, in *The Collected Works* (New York: Alfred A. Knopf, 2007), 48.

3. Kahlil Gibran to Mary Haskell, November 7, 1918, in *Beloved Prophet: The Love Letters of Kahlil Gibran and Mary Haskell and Her Private Journal*, ed. Virginia Hilu (New York: Alfred A. Knopf, 1972), 318.

4. Barbara Young to Marianna Gibran, May 14, 1945, Soumaya Museum, Mexico City.

5. Mary Haskell's journal, August 31, 1920, in *Beloved Prophet,* 343.

6. Kahlil Gibran, *Secrets of the Heart: Poems and Meditations,* ed. Martin Wolf, trans. Anthony R. Ferris (1947; repr., Secaucus, NJ: Citadel Press, 1975), 5.

7. Ibid., 6.

8. Ibid., 8.

9. Ibid., 9.

10. Ibid.

11. Ibid., 10.

12. Ibid., 15.

13. Ibid., 21–22.

14. Ibid., 23.

15. Amin Maalouf, *Leo Africanus,* trans. Peter Sluglett (1986, trans., Chicago: New Amsterdam Books, 1988), 103.

16. Gibran, *Secrets of the Heart,* 24–25.

17. *Ancient Christian Commentary on Scripture: New Testament VI,* ed. Gerald Bray (Chicago: Fitzroy Dearborn, 1998), 321.

18. Kahlil Gibran to May Ziadah, October 5, 1923, in *Love Letters: The Love Letters of Kahlil Gibran to May Ziadah,* eds. and trans. Suheil Bushrui and Salma Haffar Al-Kuzbari (1983; repr., Oxford: Oneworld, 2008), 107.

19. Gibran, *Secrets of the Heart,* 214–15.

20. Gibran to Ziadah, February 7, 1919, in *Love Letters,* 14.

21. Gibran, *Secrets of the Heart,* 226–27.

22. Kahlil Gibran, *The Prophet* (1923; repr., New York: Alfred A. Knopf, 1992), 50.

23. Kahlil Gibran, *Poems, Parables and Drawings* (New York: Dover, 2008), 170.

Chapter 6: The Prophet

1. Kahlil Gibran, *The Prophet* (1923; repr., New York: Alfred A. Knopf, 1992), 93.

2. Suheil Bushrui and Joe Jenkins, *Kahlil Gibran: Man and Poet: A New Biography* (1998; repr., Oxford: Oneworld, 1999), 224.

3. Jean Gibran and Kahlil Gibran, *Kahlil Gibran: His Life and World* (1974; repr., New York: Interlink, 1998), 371.

4. Barbara Young, *This Man from Lebanon: A Study of Kahlil Gibran* (New York: Alfred A. Knopf, 1945), ix.

5. Gibran and Gibran, *His Life and World,* 360.

6. Alexandre Najjar, *Kahlil Gibran: A Biography* (London: Saqi, 2008), 160.

7. Mikhail Naimy, *Kahlil Gibran: A Biography* (1934; repr., New York: Philosophical Society, 1985), 194.

8. Young, *This Man from Lebanon*, 16.

9. Bushrui, *Man and Poet*, 330.

10. Kahlil Gibran, "The Future of the Arabic Language," quoted in "From 'The Future of the Arabic Language,'" trans. Adnan Haydar, *Tablet and Pen: Writings from the Modern Middle East,* November 2010, http://www.wordswithoutborders.org/article/from-the-future-of-the-arabic-language.

11. Gibran, *The Prophet*, 1.

12. Ibid.

13. Ibid., 9, 10.

14. Ibid., 11, 12.

15. Ibid., 13.

16. Ibid., 26, 28.

17. Ibid., 29.

18. Ibid., 50, 51.

19. Ibid., 52, 53.

20. Ibid., 78, 79.

21. Ibid., 80, 81.

22. Daniel Rondeau, *L'Express,* November 28, 2002, http://www.najjar.org/en/khalil_Gibran_en.asp.

23. Gibran and Gibran, *His Life and World*, 314.

24. Gibran, quoted in Mary Haskell's journal, May 6, 1918, in *Beloved Prophet: The Love Letters of Kahlil Gibran and Mary Haskell and Her Private Journal,* ed. Virginia Hilu (New York: Alfred A. Knopf, 1972), 303.

25. Najjar, *Kahlil Gibran*, 142, 148.

26. Haskell to Gibran, October 2, 1923, in *Beloved Prophet,* 416–17.

27. Suheil Bushrui, interview by author, June 2010.

28. Young, *This Man from Lebanon*, 97.

29. Najjar, *Kahlil Gibran*, 150.

30. Ibid., 141.

31. Kahlil Gibran, *A Tear and a Smile,* in *The Collected Works* (New York: Alfred A. Knopf, 2007), 878.

32. Najjar, *Kahlil Gibran*, 83.

33. Ameen Rihani, *A Chant of Mystics and Other Poems*, eds. S. B. Bushrui and J. Munro (Beirut: Rihani House, 1970), 106.

34. Retrieved from: http://4umi.com/gibran/thought/.

35. Bushrui, *Man and Poet*, 100.

36. Gibran, *Sand and Foam*, in *Collected Works*, 176.

37. Ibid., 177.

38. Wahib Kayrouz, interview by author, Bsharri, Lebanon, February 2008.

39. Wahib Kayrouz, *Gibran in His Museum*, trans. Alfred Murr (Lebanon: Gibran Museum, 2003), 96.

40. Gibran, quoted in Mary Haskell's journal, June 16, 1923, in *Beloved Prophet*, 412.

Chapter 7: The Son of Man

1. Suheil Bushrui and Joe Jenkins, *Kahlil Gibran: Man and Poet: A New Biography* (1998; repr., Oxford: Oneworld, 1999), 9.

2. Wahib Kayrouz, *Gibran in His Museum,* trans. Alfred Murr (Lebanon: Gibran Museum, 2003), 103.

3. Tarif Khalidi, "Jesus through Muslim Eyes," BBC, September 3, 2009, http://www.bbc.co.uk/religion/religions/islam/beliefs/isa.shtml.

4. Barbara Young, *This Man from Lebanon: A Study of Kahlil Gibran* (New York: Alfred A. Knopf, 1945), 95–96.

5. Ibid., 97.

6. Mahatma Gandhi, "What Jesus Means to Me," *Modern Review*, October 1941, 406.

7. E. Stanley Jones, *Gandhi: Portrayal of a Friend* (Nashville: Abingdon Press, 1993), 143.

8. Mikhail Naimy, *Kahlil Gibran: A Biography* (1934; repr., New York: Philosophical Society, 1985), 207–8.

9. Ibid., 211.

10. Alexandre Najjar, *Kahlil Gibran: A Biography* (London: Saqi, 2008), 72.

11. Ibid., 79.

12. Jean Gibran and Kahlil Gibran, *Kahlil Gibran: His Life and World* (1974; repr., New York: Interlink, 1998), 384–85.

13. Naimy, *Kahlil Gibran*, 209.

14. Gibran and Gibran, *His Life and World*, 166.

15. Bushrui, *Man and Poet*, 256.

16. Young, *This Man from Lebanon*, 170, 171.

17. Ibid., 110.

18. Kahlil Gibran, *Jesus the Son of Man* (1928; repr., New York: Alfred A. Knopf, 1995), 132, 55.

19. Ibid., 16–18.

20. Ibid., 19.

21. Ibid., 20.

22. Ibid., 46.

23. Ibid.

24. Ibid., 50.

25. Ibid., 52–53.

26. Ibid., 54–55.

27. Ibid., 80.

28. Ibid., 86.

29. Ibid., 98.

30. Ibid., 141.

31. Ibid., 256.

32. Najjar, *Kahlil Gibran*, 72.

33. Bushrui, *Man and Poet*, 251.

34. Kahlil Gibran, *The Crucified,* in *The Treasured Writings of Kahlil Gibran*, ed. Martin L. Wolf, trans. Anthony R. Ferris (Edison, NJ: Citadel Press, 1951), 229.

35. Young, *This Man from Lebanon*, 106.

36. Ibid.

37. Kahlil Gibran, quoted in Mary Haskell's journal, January 10, 1914, in *Beloved Prophet: The Love Letters of Kahlil Gibran and Mary Haskell and Her Private Journal*, ed. Virginia Hilu (New York: Alfred A. Knopf, 1972), 167.

38. Kahlil Gibran, *Sand and Foam*, in *The Collected Works* (New York: Alfred A. Knopf, 2007), 194.

39. Gibran, quoted in Mary Haskell's journal, January 7, 1920, in *Beloved Prophet*, 349.

40. Najjar, *Kahlil Gibran*, 157.

41. Gibran, quoted in Mary Haskell's journal, January 6, 1918, in *Beloved Prophet*, 294.

42. Gibran, *Sand and Foam*, in *Collected Works*, 223.

Chapter 8: The Wanderer

1. Kahlil Gibran, *Sand and Foam,* in *The Collected Works* (New York: Alfred A. Knopf, 2007), 211.

2. Kahlil Gibran, *The Prophet* (1923; repr., New York: Alfred A. Knopf, 1992), 82.

3. Mikhail Naimy, *Kahlil Gibran: A Biography* (1934; repr., New York: Philosophical Society, 1985), 216.

4. Jean Gibran and Kahlil Gibran, *Kahlil Gibran: His Life and World* (1974; repr., New York: Interlink, 1998), 397.

5. Naimy, *Kahlil Gibran*, 254, 255.

6. Ibid., 227.

7. Gibran, *The Earth Gods,* in *Collected Works,* 428.

8. Gibran, *The Garden of the Prophet,* in *Collected Works,* 536, 540, 554.

9. Ibid., 533.

10. Ibid., 534.

11. Kahlil Gibran, *Lazarus and His Beloved: A One-Act Play* (London: William Heinemann, 1973).

12. Gibran, *The Wanderer,* in *Collected Works,* 459.

13. Ibid., 502.

14. Amin Maalouf, *Leo Africanus,* trans. Peter Sluglett (1986, trans., Chicago: New Amsterdam Books, 1988), 1.

15. Retrieved from: http://baabamaal.tv/biography/.

16. Barbara Young, *This Man from Lebanon: A Study of Kahlil Gibran* (New York: Alfred A. Knopf, 1945), 168.

17. Ibid., 3.

18. Gibran, *Sand and Foam,* in *Collected Works,* 227.

19. Young, *This Man from Lebanon,* 147.

20. Gibran and Gibran, *His Life and World,* 407.

21. Ibid., 408.

22. Young, *This Man from Lebanon,* 151.

23. Robin Waterfield, *Prophet: The Life and Times of Kahlil Gibran* (New York: St. Martin's, 1998), 173–174.

24. Naimy, *Kahlil Gibran,* 231.

25. Kahlil Gibran to Mary Haskell, November 17, 1918, in *Beloved Prophet: The Love Letters of Kahlil Gibran and Mary Haskell and Her Private Journal,* ed. Virginia Hilu (New York: Alfred A. Knopf, 1972), 319.

26. Gibran, *The Wanderer,* in *Collected Works,* 511.

Chapter 9: A Man for Our Times

1. Kahlil Gibran, *Jesus the Son of Man* (1928; repr., New York: Alfred A. Knopf, 1995), 183.

2. Mahmoud Darwish, "Think of Others," in *Almond Blossoms and Beyond,* trans. Mohammad Shaheen (Northampton, MA: Interlink Books, 2009), 3.

3. Reynold A. Nicholson, ed., *Selected Poems from the Divani Shamsi Tabriz* (London: Cambridge University Press, 1898), 121–31.

4. Kahlil Gibran, *Spiritual Sayings of Kahlil Gibran,* ed. and trans. Anthony R. Ferris (1962; repr., Secaucus, NJ: Citadel Press, 1976), 39.

5. Kahlil Gibran, *The Garden of the Prophet,* in *The Collected Works* (New York: Alfred A. Knopf, 2007), 540.

6. Ibid., 226.

7. Ibid., 212.

8. Kahlil Gibran, *Poems, Parables and Drawings* (New York: Dover, 2008), 155.

9. Retrieved from: http://www.poemhunter.com/poem/the-bridge-55/.

10. Kahlil Gibran, "The New Frontier," in *The Treasured Writings of Kahlil Gibran*, ed. Martin L. Wolf, trans. Anthony R. Ferris (Edison, NJ: Citadel Press, 1951), 778.

11. Kahlil Gibran, quoted in Mary Haskell's journal, December 25, 1912, in *Beloved Prophet: The Love Letters of Kahlil Gibran and Mary Haskell and Her Private Journal*, ed. Virginia Hilu (New York: Alfred A. Knopf, 1972), 112.

12. Gibran, *Poems, Parables and Drawings*, 188.

13. Mikhail Naimy, *Kahlil Gibran: A Biography* (1934; repr., New York: Philosophical Society, 1985), 264.

14. Ibid., 246.

Index

About the Author

Paul-Gordon Chandler is the bishop of the Episcopal Church in Wyoming. He grew up in Senegal, West Africa, and has lived and worked extensively around the world in senior leadership roles within faith-based publishing, the arts, relief and development and The Episcopal Church. An author, art curator, social entrepreneur and an authority on the Middle East and Africa, he is passionate about using the arts to further our global quest for a more harmonious future, both with each other and with the earth. In 2020, he was awarded by the Archbishop of Canterbury the Hubert Walter Award for Reconciliation and Interfaith Cooperation, the highest international award for outstanding service in the work of reconciliation and interfaith dialogue within the Anglican Communion. The author of several books, his acclaimed book on Muslim-Christian relations is *Pilgrims of Christ on the Muslim Road: Exploring a New Path Between Two Faiths* (Rowman & Littlefield).

He can be reached at paulgordonchandler.com